KU-538-467

Making Antique Quilts

Rita Weiss

Sterling Publishing Co., Inc.
New York

Project Co-ordinator: Joyce Lerner
Technical Editor: Ann Harnden
Diagrams: Annette Stockley
Photography: Wayne Norton
Photo Stylist: Carol Wilson Mansfield
Book Design: Joyce Lerner
Produced by The Creative Partners™, LLC.

Acknowledgments

Many thanks to the following companies for supplying fabrics
for several of the samples:

Northcott Silk Inc., for Artisan's Palette by Ro Gregg used in Grecian Square
Westminster Fabrics for Fruit Basket by Kaffe Fassett used in Broken Wheel
RJR Fabrics for Vintage Violets by Debbie Beaves used in Kite Flowers
Timeless Treasures for Victoriana by Pat Campbell used in Hexagon Illusion

The following companies supplied swatches of reproduction fabrics
available today:

Windham Fabrics, a division of Baum Textile Mills
RJR Fabrics
Marcus Brothers Textiles
Robert Kaufman Fine Fabrics

Most of the quilts were photographed at the
Escondido Historical Society, Escondido, California

Library of Congress Cataloging-in-Publication Data Available

10 9 8 7 6 5 4 3 2 1

Published in paperback in 2007 by Sterling Publishing Co., Inc.
387 Park Avenue South, New York, NY 10016
© 2005 by The Creative Partners, LLC™
Distributed in Canada by Sterling Publishing
C/o Canadian Manda Group, 165 Dufferin Street
Toronto, Ontario, Canada M6K 3H6
Distributed in the United Kingdom by GMC Distribution Services
Castle Place, 166 High Street, Lewes, East Sussex, England BN7 1XU
Distributed in Australia by Capricorn Link (Australia) Pty. Ltd.
P.O. Box 704, Windsor, NSW 2756, Australia

Printed in China
All rights reserved

Sterling ISBN-13: 978-1-4027-2317-9 Hardcover
        ISBN-10: 1-4027-2317-2
        ISBN-13: 978-1-4027-4742-7 Paperback
        ISBN-10: 1-4027-4742-X

For information about custom editions, special sales, premium
and corporate purchases, please contact Sterling Special Sales
Department at 800-805-5489 or specialsales@sterlingpub.com

*I*ntroduction

If you are as fascinated with quilts as I am, join me on this trip back into history to visit with some unknown quiltmakers and their beautiful works of art. Here you will find a treasure trove of quilts made from 1850 to 1940, including some of the most beloved ones.

This book would never have been possible without the help of two dear quilting friends of mine: Lee Grover and Christina Jensen. Both ladies love antique quilts as much as I do. In fact, many of the quilts in this book come from their personal collections. Besides being collectors and lovers of quilts, both ladies have the uncanny ability to discern how a quilt was actually made. Without their help and guidance, I could never have written the instructions for recreating these antique quilts. Together, the three of us were able to start on a wonderful journey. As we examined the antique quilts we found many fascinating details about them. For instance, most of the antique quilts were self-bound either by bringing the backing to the front or by placing the sides together, stitching all around and turning right side out. We used none of these methods in our instructions for the quilts because today it is much more common to add separate bindings on quilts.

When we began I wanted to present a quilt for each decade, but both Lee and Christina convinced me that we would give rise to many more questions than answers. Since we do not know who made these quilts or the dates of their creation, we can only make an educated guess as to the exact time a quilt was made. We decided, therefore, to divide the book in half. The first section deals with quilts made between 1850 and 1900 and the second section involves quilts made up to 1940.

As you examine the quilts shared in this book, you will find that each one differs in pattern, fabrics and colors. You may choose to reproduce any one of these quilts using the reproduction fabrics currently available, which appear as close to the original colors as possible. Or, you may decide to make your own version of a Give It a Try section for each quilt. Whatever you decide, we know that like us, you will find yourself wondering how women of this time period managed to introduce quilting into their hard and busy daily lives.

4

CONTENTS

BROKEN WHEEL 76

GRECIAN SQUARE 100

JACOB'S LADDER 120

DOUBLE WEDDING RING 84

HEXAGON BOUQUETS 106

KITE FLOWERS 126

FRAMED NINE-PATCH 94

HEXAGON ILLUSIONS 114

POTTED POSIES 134

WHEEL OF FORTUNE 142

1850-1900 *Quilts*

With the introduction of aniline dyes in the mid-1800s and the proliferation of manufactured fabrics later in this period, fabrics became more readily available to home sewers. Add to this mix the availability of published patterns, the migration West and the completion of the Intercontinental Railway System, and quilters became able to make quilts from yardage instead of worn clothing.

New dyes helped prevent deterioration of fabrics made with madder dyes and a tin mordant. The tin

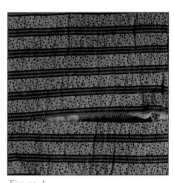

Figure 1

was used to set the colors, but over time it caused fabrics to become brittle, split and rot or for whole sections to disappear as in Figure 1. Turkey red cottons were favorites of quilters because they were colorfast and wore well. Green, yellow and red calicos, shown in Figure 2, were very popular and were

Figure 2

manufactured from the 1830s through the 1930s. But the color combination used most often in this period was indigo blue and white, shown in Figure 3.

Figure 3

Women had been using this pairing for many years in clothing and coverlets. The indigo dye was known to be unusually colorfast, and it was widely available from fabric manufacturers. Women were happy to make quilts that would still look good after many washings.

Another boon to quilters during this period was the introduction of the home sewing machine. The first practical machine was developed in 1846 by Elias Howe in an attempt to ease his wife's workload. However, the cost of this machine ($125) and others introduced during this decade was prohibitive for most women when a household's average annual income was only $500. It wasn't until 1856 when Isaac Merritt Singer offered his machines to families on a payment plan that quiltmakers found themselves with a tool that freed up time from making clothing and allowed them to become more prolific in making quilts. These new machines were so popular that it is estimated that between 50 and 75 percent of the quilts made after 1870 included some machine stitching in either piecing or in applying the binding. Oddly enough, the only quilt in this section that has any machine stitching is the Log Cabin Trails shown in Figure 4. The quiltmaker (or someone else at a later time) machine-stitched a cable design on the borders of the

Figure 4

quilt, even though the blocks were all hand-stitched. The rest of the quilts included here were pieced and quilted entirely by hand.

As can be seen in the quilts in this section, earlier quilts of this period were made mainly of scraps due in large part to the Civil War. Women dedicated themselves to sending their husbands, fathers, brothers and sons off to war with a warm quilt – many of them undoubtedly family heirlooms relinquished to the desperation of the times. Quilts were made by aid societies to use in fundraising with blocks and fabrics received from many different sources. Women of both the North and South quickly began making quilts with whatever fabric was available and sent them off to the front in their attempt to provide relief from the hardships of the war. Even after the war ended, fabric was in scarce supply to most women, especially those in the South. It took several years for the economy to recover during which time women continued to use any salvageable fabric to keep their families in bed-coverings.

As financial times improved in the last 25 years of this period, quilts became more intricate, more colorful, more creative and often used planned fabric yardage. Appliqué gained a new popularity in indi-

Figure 5

vidual blocks, instead of as a central medallion, and was often rendered in red, green and white as in Figure 5. Pieced-basket designs showed up in many quilts (Figure 6), the Log Cabin pattern appeared in quilts shortly after the Civil War (Figure 7) and Crazy Quilts became the rage. Quiltmakers from

Figure 6

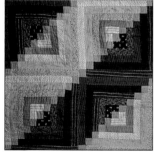
Figure 7

this period still made quilts for practical purposes, many of which are today found in faded-and-worn condition. But, they increasingly were able to make quilts for the joy of it. Many of these quilts were packed away "for best" and are often found today in pristine, like-new condition.

Quilt patterns spread across the country as families migrated west. Pattern names and designs changed as the quiltmaker attempted to relate them to new experiences and new objects in her life. Published quilt patterns also added to the proliferation of quilts made during the last decades of this period. The Ladies Art Co. began printing patterns in 1889 in their *Diagrams of Quilt, Sofa and Pincushion Patterns*. Other publications of the time, such as *Hearth and Home, The Household, Arthur's Home Magazine, The Ohio Farmer, Comfort, Godey's Lady Book* and *Ladies Home Companion*, regularly included quilt patterns. Each publication gave names to the designs contained in its pages. These included patterns in use for many years and even those in other current publications that were simply renamed. Quilt patterns popular over many years can be found today with as many as 15-20 different names.

When the country look became popular in the 1980s and magazines began showing antique quilts as decorator items, antique collectors began adding quilts to their wish list. Quilts from this period were often found in dark, warm colors or in the timeless combinations of blue and white or red and white making them much sought after by collectors. Quiltmaking itself also saw a resurgence in popularity as quilters rushed to make their own versions of these old beauties. As this trend continued to grow, fabric manufacturers were quick to add reproduction fabrics to their inventories. Quilters who want to imitate quilts from this period are enjoying the availability of fabrics just like the originals – many in the exact prints with colors as close to the original as possible. Judie Rothermel, Barbara Brackman, Terry Clothier Thompson, Jo Morton, Harriet Hargraves and Mary Koval have designed many lines of reproduction fabrics specific to quilts of this 1850-1900 period (Figure 8).

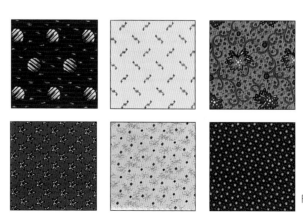
Figure 8

Broken Star

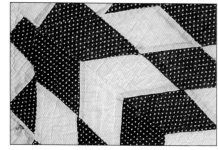
Figure 1

Typical of the 1860s era, navy-with-white dots combines with solid white to create an eye-catching quilt. This color combination is much sought after by collectors. Star designs are especially popular. This Broken Star quilt has an unusual setting and is not constructed in blocks. Four pieced star points are joined with a square. These units are then joined with large squares and side triangles to piece the entire top. An alternate piecing method used in Give It A Try does result in one large block or a quarter of the whole quilt.

The quiltmaker did a great job of piecing the star-design center, but her borders were not carefully planned. She may have tried to cut triangles whose base was the same size as the side of one of the small diamond pieces, but as she added the triangles to the sides of the quilt, she discovered that did not work out evenly. That meant when she got to the corners, she did not end up with a complete piece as shown in the close-up of one corner (Figure 1). She solved her problem by simply trimming them off.

We found a similar problem when drafting the border triangles. Although we could draft a piece that would fit perfectly along the edges to align with the star pieces, it would have meant making two different border triangles. We decided that would be too confusing, so we drafted the triangles to fit the sides to create perfect corners, but we cannot match the border triangles with the edges of the star pieces. In the 1800s, drafting such a pattern must have been difficult. We also discovered that on the original quilt, the triangles all have long bias edges that are easy to stretch when stitching pieces together. This quilt does not look stretched as all sides appear equal, and it lies flat, but it has been washed and is well worn, so it could be that whatever problems there were shrunk out.

Although the original quilt was probably made using templates with pieces being cut one at a time, in today's quilting world, it is easy to join strips to cut units, saving time in both cutting and piecing.

Figure 2

The original quilt was quilted in the ditch of the star-unit seams and in a 1" grid throughout the remainder of the quilt (Figure 2).

No matter what fabrics or methods you choose to construct your quilt, you can't lose making this beautiful Broken Star design.

MAKE THE ANTIQUE QUILT

Finished Quilt Size 78" square

MATERIALS

Based on 42" fabric width.

Navy-with-white dots 2½ yards

White solid 5¾ yards

Backing 5 yards

Batting 84" square

Coordinating thread

Rotary-cutting tools with ruler
    with 45-degree angle markings

CUTTING INSTRUCTIONS

Refer to Diagram 1 for cutting squares into triangles.

Diagram 1

Navy-with-white dots–fabric-width strips

- 25 strips 2" for B
- 3 strips 3¾"; cut strips into twenty-four 3¾" squares. Cut squares on both diagonals to make 96 F triangles.
- 8 strips 2¼" for binding

White solid–fabric-width strips

- 20 strips 2" for A
- 3 strips 3¾"; cut strip into twenty-five 3¾" squares. Cut squares on both diagonals to make 100 G triangles
- 3 strips 6⅞"; cut into sixteen 6⅞" C squares.
- 2 strips 13¼"; cut into four 13¼" D squares.
- 1 strip 19¼"; cut into two 19¼" squares. Cut each square on both diagonals to make 4 E triangles.

White solid–along the length of fabric

- 2 strips 7½" x 64½" for H
- 2 strips 7½" x 78½" for I

Use ¼" seam allowance for piecing. Arrows indicate pressing direction.

PIECING THE STAR UNITS

1. Sew an A strip to a B strip to an A strip with right sides together along length; press. Repeat for five pieced strips.

2. Using a rotary ruler, cut one end of one pieced strip at a 45-degree angle (Diagram 2).

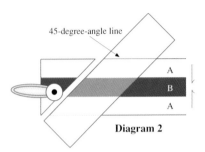

45-degree-angle line

A
B
A

Diagram 2

3. Cut 2" segments from the remainder of the strip (Diagram 3); repeat for all strips to create 64 A-B-A units.

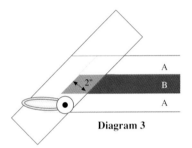

2"

A
B
A

Diagram 3

4. Sew a B strip to an A strip to a B strip; press seams toward B. Repeat for 10 pieced strips.

5. Repeat steps 2 and 3 to make 128 B-A-B units (Diagram 4).

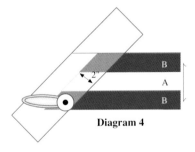

2"

B
A
B

Diagram 4

6. Join one A-B-A unit with two B-A-B units to complete a star unit (Diagram 5); press. Repeat for 64 star units.

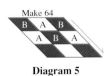

Make 64

| B | A | B |
| A | B | A |

Diagram 5

7. Mark the seam allowance at the points of each B piece (Diagram 6).

Diagram 6

ASSEMBLING THE TOP

1. Join two star units to make a star point, stopping stitching at the marked seam allowance (Diagram 7); press. Repeat for 32 star points.

Make 32

Diagram 7

2. Pin a C square to one inside angle of one star point and stitch from the end of the outside seam allowance to the center, stopping at the marked seam allowance; secure seam at both ends. (Diagram 8).

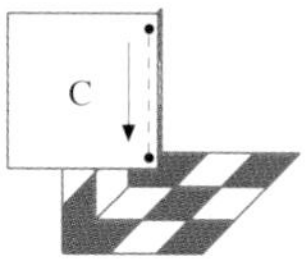

Diagram 8

3. Repeat on the opposite inside angle (Diagram 9); press.

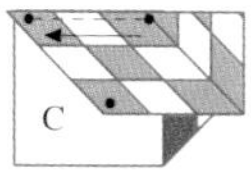

Diagram 9

4. Set the remaining sides of C into a second star point as in steps 2 and 3 to complete a C unit (Diagram 10); press seams away from C. Repeat for 16 C units.

Diagram 10

5. Join four C units with D as in steps 2 and 3 to make a D unit (Diagram 11); press seams away from D. Repeat for two D units.

Diagram 11

6. Join two C units with E as in steps 2 and 3 to make an E unit (Diagram 12); press. Repeat for four E units.

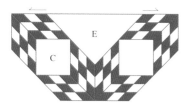

Diagram 12

7. Join the D and E units with the remaining D squares and E triangles as in steps 2 and 3 (Diagram 13), to complete the quilt center; press seams away from D and E.

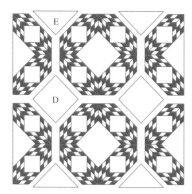

Diagram 13

8. Sew F triangle to G triangle along short edges (Diagram 14). Continue to join F and G pieces to make four strips each with 24 F and 25 G triangles, beginning and ending with G. Press seams toward F.

Diagram 14

9. Sew an F-G strip to each side of the quilt center, joining G pieces at corners (Diagram 15); press seams toward F-G strips.

Diagram 15

10. Sew an H strip to opposite sides and I strips to the top and bottom of the quilt center; press seams toward H and I strips.

FINISHING

1. Piece backing to create an 84" square.

2. Mark top for quilting, sandwich quilt layers, hand- or machine-quilt and bind edges referring to the General Quiltmaking Instructions. The quilt shown was quilted in the ditch of star-unit seams and in a 1" grid throughout the remainder of the quilt.

Broken Star
Assembly Diagram 78" Square

Give It A Try...

Use black for the background and bright-colored fabrics for the star points to show this pattern in a whole new way. The sample is pieced with four 16" blocks. The blocks were created by dividing the D and E triangles in the quilt into two triangles each. Part of the construction process remains the same as the C squares are still set into the star units. But joining the four blocks to create one large star motif, or one quarter of the quilt center, makes joining the units easy.

- To make the four-block sample, cut three strips yellow, five strips blue and seven strips red mottleds 2" by width of fabric.

- From black solid, cut four 67/8" C squares and four 97/8" E squares. Cut the E squares in half on one diagonal to make eight E triangles.

- Complete three yellow/blue/red A strips and two red/blue/red B strips cut to make star units referring to quilt instructions on page 10.

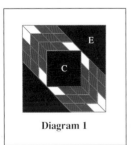

Diagram 1

- Complete four C units referring to quilt instructions on page 11.

- Sew an E triangle to each side of a C unit to complete one block. (Diagram 1); press. Repeat for four blocks.

- Join the four blocks to complete a four-block top.

- Border and finish as desired.

Buzzard's Roost

This quilt proved to be a challenge to date. It was purchased as a mid- to late-1800s quilt from a reputable antique dealer, who bought it at an old estate sale in New England. It is made of a chintz-finished white print and two brownish-green geometric prints that are so very similar in look but different in the size of the motifs (Figure 1). The color of these prints suggests mid-1800s (Figure 2), yet the backing fabric does not immediately "read" as that same era (Figure 3). Because the early quiltmaker used yardage, it is likely that the top was made all at once, unlike scrap quilts that might take years to complete.

Figure 1

Figure 2

Figure 3

It is possible that the top was a UFO (unfinished object) so common to quilters of today. Perhaps it was set aside and either picked up at a later time and finished by the quiltmaker or by one of her descendants. This would also explain the many types of binding used on this quilt. The top and binding were both turned in and stitched on two sides, a separate binding of the backing fabric was added to a third side and part of the fourth, and another fabric altogether was used for a short stretch to finish it. Perhaps the quilter ran out of fabric or the fabric intended for the binding was used for another purpose through the years. Whatever the explanation for the discrepancies in this quilt, trying to assign a date to an old quilt is a great way to develop a relationship with the quilters of the past.

MAKE THE ANTIQUE QUILT

Finished Quilt Size 79½" Square
Finished Block Size 9" Square
Number of Blocks 20

MATERIALS

Based on 42" fabric width.

Binding print ¾ yard

White print 3¼ yards

Green print 4 yards

Backing 5 yards

Batting 86" square

Coordinating thread

Rotary-cutting tools

CUTTING INSTRUCTIONS

Refer to Diagram 1 for cutting squares into triangles.

Diagram 1

Binding print–fabric-width strips

- 9 strips 2¼" or 2½" for binding

White print–fabric-width strips

- 5 strips 5"; cut into forty 5" A squares

- 6 strips 5¾"; cut into forty 5¾" squares. Cut squares on both diagonals to make 160 B triangles.

- 7 strips 3⅛"; cut into eighty 3⅛" squares. Cut squares on 1 diagonal to make 160 C triangles.

- 2 strips 14"; cut into five 14" squares. Cut squares on both diagonals to make 20 M triangles.

Green print–fabric-width strips

- 7 strips 3⅛"; cut into eighty 3⅛" squares. Cut squares on 1 diagonal to make 160 D triangles.

- 6 strips 5¾"; cut into forty 5¾" squares. Cut squares on both diagonals to make 160 E triangles.

- 27 strips 2¾"; cut 12 strips into forty-eight 2¾" x 9½" F rectangles. Set aside remaining strips for sashing.

Use ¼" seam allowance for piecing. Arrows indicate pressing direction.

PIECING THE BLOCKS

1. Sew D to adjacent short sides of B and press (Diagram 2). Repeat to make 80 B-D units.

2. Sew B-D to opposite sides of A and press to make a block center row (Diagram 3). Repeat to make 40 center rows.

Diagram 2

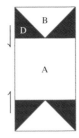

Diagram 3

3. Sew E to adjacent short sides of B and press (Diagram 4).

Diagram 4

4. Add C to each end of a B-E unit to complete a block side row (Diagram 5); press. Repeat to make 80 side rows.

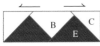

Diagram 5

5. Sew a side row to each side of a center row to complete one block referring to the Block Diagram; press seams toward the center rows. Repeat to make 40 blocks.

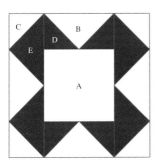

Block Diagram
9" Square
Make 40

ASSEMBLING THE TOP

Refer to the Assembly Diagram on page 18 as needed for the following instructions.

1. Join the blocks in rows with F (Diagram 6); press seams toward F.

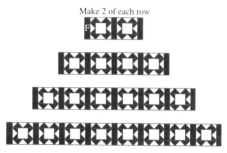

Make 2 of each row

Diagram 6

2. Join the sashing strips on short ends to make a long strip; press seams to one side. Cut into sashing strips as follows: two 12" G, two 25¼" H, two 47¾" I, two 70¼" J, two 92¾" K and one 116" L.

3. Sew a sashing strip to each block row (Diagram 7); press seams toward the sashing strips. Be sure ends of sashing strips align with F ends of block rows.

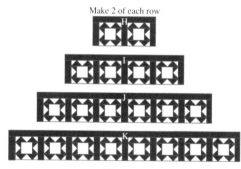

Make 2 of each row

Diagram 7

4. Sew an M triangle to each end of each block/sashing row, matching the square corner of M with the unsashed edge of the block row (Diagram 8); press. M will be shorter than the edge of the block row.

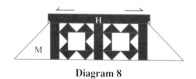

Diagram 8

5. Fold each sashed row in half across width; crease to mark center. Join one each H, I, J and K sashed rows, matching center creases and aligning the F strips from one row to the next to create straight lines (Diagram 9); press seams toward sashing strips. Repeat with remaining sashed rows.

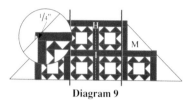

Diagram 9

6. Fold the L strip in half and crease. Center and stitch to the long edge of one pieced section allowing the L ends to extend beyond the K sashed-row ends (Diagram 10); press seam toward L.

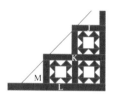

Diagram 10

7. Center and stitch the remaining pieced section on the remaining edge of L, again aligning the F strips across the L strip and allowing the L ends to extend beyond the K sashed-row ends (Diagram 11); press seam toward L.

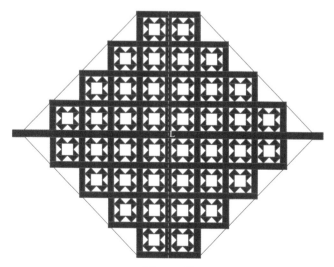

Diagram 11

8. Sew a G strip between two M triangles, aligning the square corner of M with the square end
of G (Diagram 12); press. Repeat to make two
G-M units. Crease to mark center of each unit.

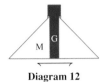

Diagram 12

9. Center and sew a G-M unit to opposite H
edges of the pieced section, aligning G with
the F strip across the H strip (Diagram 13);
press.

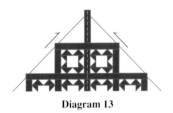

Diagram 13

10. Using a rotary cutter and large acrylic square;
trim L and G ends even with the M triangles to
create square corners (Diagram 14). Trim ends
of sashing strips even with M triangles along
each side using a long rotary ruler.

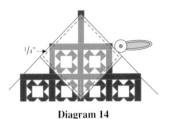

Diagram 14

FINISHING

1. Piece backing to create an 86" square.

2. Mark top for quilting, sandwich quilt layers,
hand- or machine-quilt and bind edges referring to the General Quiltmaking Instructions.

Buzzard's Roost Variation
Assembly Diagram 79½" Square

Give It A Try...

Make a small sample to give this pattern a try. Use a straight set instead of the diagonal set of the antique quilt and eliminate the sashing to give the design a very different look.

- Referring to quilt Cutting Instructions on page 16, cut 4 A squares, 5 B squares and 10 C squares from light fabric. Cut 14 D squares, 4 E squares and 4 border strips 2¾" x 14" from dark fabric. Cut squares into triangles as directed.

- Complete four blocks referring to the Block Diagram and Piecing the Blocks instructions on page 16. Join the blocks in two rows and join the rows to complete the center.

- Stitch four more B-D units.

- Sew a C triangle to a D triangle along the diagonal; press seam toward D. Repeat to make four C-D units.

- Sew a B-D unit to each end of two border strips and a C-D unit to each end of the remaining border strips (Diagram 1); press.

- Sew the C-D strips to opposite sides of the center; press seams toward strips.

- Sew the B-D strips to the remaining sides of the center to complete the sample; press seam towards strips.

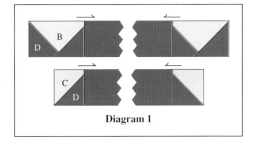

Diagram 1

Chimney Sweep Variation

The Chimney Sweep Variation antique quilt is easy to make if the block is made using corner triangles to make square blocks as demonstrated in Give It A Try. The way the antique quilt is

stitched, the blocks are not square, but have angled corners, making it impossible to join the blocks in rows. The setting squares are all made with a stripe fabric (Figure 1). It would not have been easy to cut triangles from the stripe and sew them together with all stripes matching. For this reason, the antique quilt could not have been made using the easier method of block piecing.

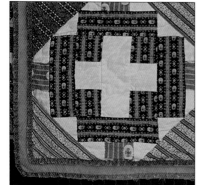

Figure 1

It is interesting to note that most of the blocks in this quilt were made with only one dark fabric, but there were a few blocks that had a couple of different dark pieces added. Note the different fabric added at the top right corner in Figure 2. It may be that the quiltmaker did not have enough fabric to complete the block, or she knew that one day quiltmakers would be wondering about her decisions. Wherever she is, she is getting a chuckle out of our speculations about her wonderful quilt.

Figure 2

MAKE THE ANTIQUE QUILT

Finished Quilt Size 70" x 87½"
Finished Block Size 7" Square
Number of Blocks 80

MATERIALS

Based on 42" fabric width.

Binding print ¾ yard

Tan print 2½ yards

Stripe 2¾ yards

Total assorted dark prints 3¼ yards

Backing 6 yards

Batting 76" x 94"

Coordinating thread

Rotary-cutting tools

CUTTING INSTRUCTIONS

Refer to Diagram 1 to cut squares into triangles.

Diagram 1

Binding print–fabric-width strips

- 10 strips 2¼" or 2½" for binding

Tan print–fabric-width strips

- 7 strips 1¾" for B

- 4 strips 4¼"; cut into eighty 1¾" A rectangles.

- 18 strips 3"; cut into two-hundred-forty 3" squares. Cut squares on both diagonals to make 960 E triangles.

Assorted dark prints–fabric-width strips

If using the same dark fabric, multiple strips may be cut. The total number of strips and pieces needed is listed here. Divide these totals by the total number of different fabrics to be used to determine how many pieces of each fabric are needed.

- 28 strips 1¾" for C; cut 14 of the strips into three-hundred-twenty 1¾" C squares (4 C squares per block). Set aside remaining strips for B-C units.

- 14 strips 4¼"; cut into three-hundred-twenty 1¾" D rectangles (4 per block)

Stripe-fabric-width strips

- 9 strips 5¾"; cut into sixty-three 5¾" F squares.

- 2 squares 4⅝"; cut squares on one diagonal to make 4 H triangles.

- 2 strips 8¾"; cut into eight 8¾" squares. Cut squares on both diagonals to make 32 G triangles.

Use ¼" seam allowance for piecing. Arrows indicate pressing direction.

PIECING THE BLOCKS

1. Sew a C strip to each side of a B strip (Diagram 2); press. Repeat to make seven pieced strips.

2. Cut pieced strips into 160 C-B-C units (Diagram 2).

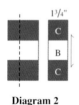

Diagram 2

3. Sew a C-B-C unit to opposite sides of A and press (Diagram 3); repeat to make 80 units.

Diagram 3

4. Sew a D rectangle to opposite sides of each A-C-B-C unit and press (Diagram 4).

Diagram 4

5. Sew E to each short end of each remaining D rectangle and to opposite sides of the remaining C squares (Diagram 5); press.

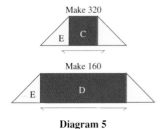

Diagram 5

6. Sew a C-E unit to the D sides of the pieced block units and press (Diagram 6).

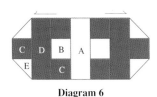

Diagram 6

7. Sew a C-E unit to each D-E unit and press (Diagram 7).

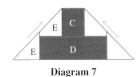

Diagram 7

8. Sew a C-E-D unit to each side of a pieced block unit to complete one block; press seams toward C-E-D units. Repeat for 80 blocks.

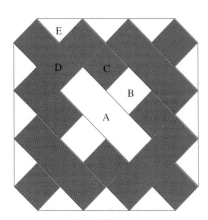

Block Diagram
7" Square
Make 80

ASSEMBLING THE TOP

Refer to the Assembly Diagram as needed for the following instructions. Because the blocks are not square and are joined with setting squares and triangles, rows cannot be easily stitched and joined.

1. Join blocks in diagonal rows with the F, G and H setting pieces (Diagram 8); press seams toward F, G and H.

Diagram 8

2. To join rows, stitch the long seam, stopping stitching at the end of the seam not at the end of the pieces. Secure stitching at end of seam, continue stitching short seam, and then back to another long seam until the rows are joined (Diagram 9); press seams in one direction.

Diagram 9

FINISHING THE QUILT

1. Piece backing to create a 76" x 94" rectangle.

2. Mark top for quilting, sandwich quilt layers, hand- or machine-quilt and bind edges referring to the General Quiltmaking Instructions.

Chimney Sweep Variation
Assembly Diagram 70" x 87½"

Give It A Try...

Use some entirely different fabrics and an easier method of joining the blocks to create another variation of this old-fashioned block.

- Referring to quilt Cutting Instructions on page 22, cut 4 A rectangles, 1 B strip, 2 C strips, 1 D strip and one E strip. Cut four 4⅝" squares each two coordinating fabrics for F and G; cut squares on one diagonal to make 8 each F and G triangles.

- Complete four blocks referring to the Alternative Block Diagram and Piecing the Blocks (page 22) instructions. Join the blocks in two rows and join the rows to complete the center.

- Add borders as desired.

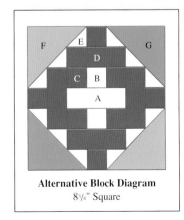

Alternative Block Diagram
8¼" Square

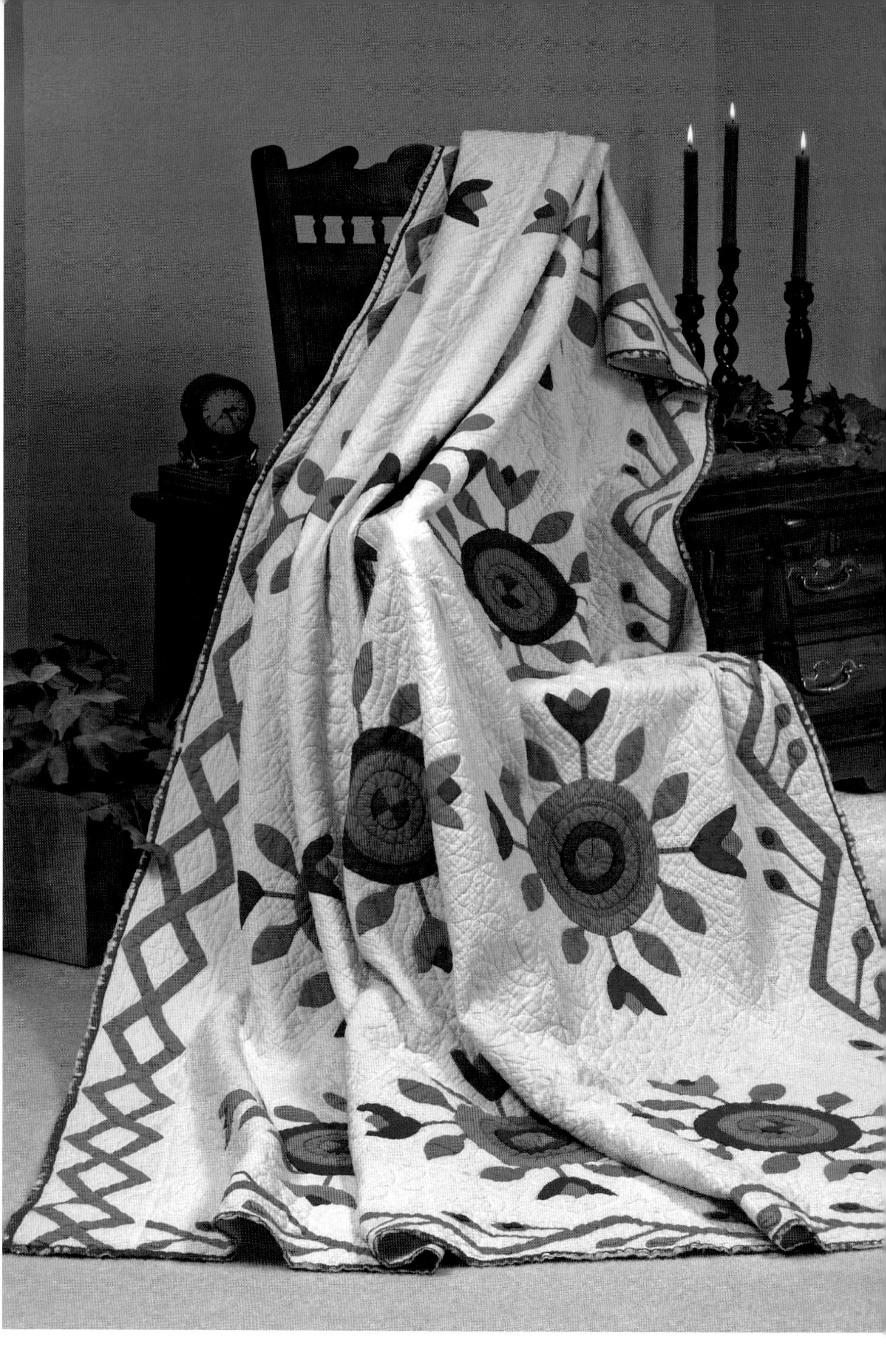

Circle Flower

The solid colors used to stitch this old appliqué quilt are worn and faded, but that has not diminished the beauty of the quilt. Appliqué quilts are less common than pieced ones, and if they were actually used, they had a tendency to wear.

This quilt has some unusual characteristics. The rings in the block centers were not appliquéd to each other; instead, they were cut in two pieces and stitched on one half at a time and then the end seams were joined (Figure 1). This would have made it possible to piece one circle shape to another. It is possible to piece circles to one another in one piece, but not easy.

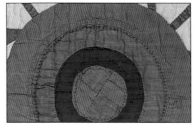

Figure 1

Another unusual characteristic is the use of two different borders. One border strip has crossed D and DR pieces (Figure 2), while the remaining borders have single D and DR pieces with appliquéd bud shapes (Figure 3). If you prefer your borders to be more balanced, create a second border strip with appliqué or make all strips with just the D and DR pieces to finish your quilt.

Figure 2

Figure 3

The antique quilt was beautifully quilted in an echo design around the appliqué shapes (Figure 4).

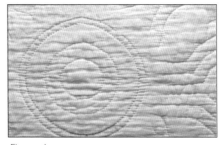

Figure 4

MAKE THE ANTIQUE QUILT

Finished Quilt Size 73¾" x 95"
Finished Block Size 15" Square
Number of Blocks 12

MATERIALS

Based on 42"-wide fabric.

Chrome orange solid 1¼ yards

Red solid 1¾ yards

Green solid 2¼ yards

Muslin 6 yards

Backing 5¾ yards

Batting 80" x 101"

Coordinating thread

Embroidery thread to match fabrics

Freezer paper

Card stock

Removable marker

5mm mechanical pencil

Rotary-cutting tools

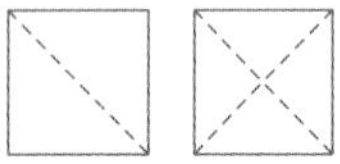

Diagram 1

CUTTING INSTRUCTIONS

Refer to Diagram 1 for cutting squares into triangles.

Muslin–fabric-length strips
(see Diagram 2 for cutting layout)

- 2 strips 5½" x 64¼" for E
- 2 strips 5½" x 95½" for F
- Eighteen 15½" A squares
- Three 22½" B squares; cut squares in half on both diagonals to make 12 B triangles. Set aside 2 triangles for another project.
- Two 11½" C squares; cut squares on 1 diagonal to make 4 C triangles.

Green solid–fabric-width strips

- 3 strips 6½" for D/DR
- 1 strip 1½" for block center piecing

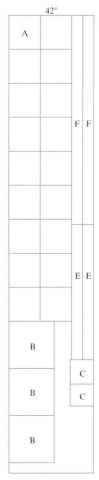

Diagram 2

- 3 strips 2¼" for stems
- Appliqué pieces as marked on patterns

Red solid–fabric width strips

- 9 strips 2¼" or 2½" for binding
- 1 strip 1½" for block center piecing
- Appliqué pieces as marked on patterns

Chrome orange solid–fabric width strips

- 2 strips 1½" for block center piecing
- Appliqué pieces as marked on patterns

Use ¼" seam allowance for piecing. Arrows indicate pressing direction.

MAKING APPLIQUÉ BLOCKS

1. Prepare templates for appliqué pieces using patterns given on pages 32 and 33.

2. Cut one of the D/DR strips in half to make two 6½" x 21" strips. Layer these two strips with wrong sides together to make a layered unit, matching edges exactly; unfold the remaining two fabric width strips and layer them wrong sides together to make a second layered unit.

3. Lay the D template on one layered strip unit, matching short edges of D to edges of strips (Diagram 3). Lay the rotary-cutting ruler on the template, matching one straight edge (Diagram 4); trim. Remove the template; continue cutting 1¼"-wide strips across the layered strips to cut D and DR pieces (Diagram 5). Repeat to cut 35 each D and DR. Set aside.

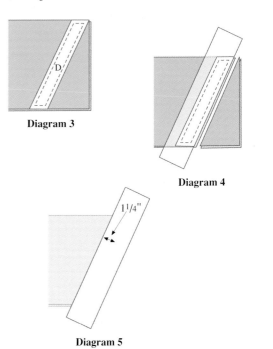

Diagram 3

Diagram 4

Diagram 5

4. Sew a 1½" green strip to a same-width orange strip with right sides together along length; press. Cut pieced strips into twelve 2½" segments (Diagram 6). Repeat with red and orange strips to make 12 segments (Diagram 6).

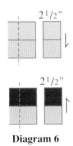

Diagram 6

5. Using the G template, cut circle pieces from the pieced segments for the pieced center units, adding ⅛"-¼" seam allowance all around.

6. Fold each stem strip with wrong sides together along length; stitch a ⅛" seam allowance. Press with seam centered on the back side of the strip (Diagram 7). Cut strips into forty-eight 2¼" stem pieces.

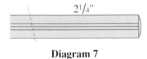

Diagram 7

7. Trace remaining pieces onto the wrong side of the fabrics referring to patterns for colors and number to cut of each shape. Cut out shapes, leaving a ⅛"-¼" turn-under allowance around each one.

8. Cut freezer-paper shapes on traced lines referring to patterns for number to cut.

9. Place a matching freezer-paper shape with dull side against the wrong side of a matching fabric shape; turn the seam allowance to the freezer-paper side and, using the tip of an iron, press the seam allowance onto the freezer paper to make a crisp edge (Diagram 8).

Freezer paper copy

Diagram 8

Repeat for all pieces with matching freezer-paper pieces. Turn under bottom edges only of H and I pieces and straight edges of K pieces. Do not turn under narrow ends of M and N pieces. Remove freezer paper.

10. Trace the entire pattern given onto a large piece of paper, adding the K and L pieces at the top of the stem. Turn paper to center a flower/leaf motif at each diagonal corner (Diagram 9). Tape the pattern to a window.

Diagram 9

11. Fold and crease each A square on the horizontal, vertical and diagonal to mark the center to help with placement of motifs.

12. Tape an A square over the pattern on the window using creased lines as guides for placement. Trace the design onto the A square using the removable marker; repeat for all A squares.

13. Place a G unit on an A square, referring to the lines marked on the background; pin and baste in place to hold. Center H on the center unit; pin and baste in place. Using thread to match H, hand-stitch in place with tiny hand stitches (Diagram 10).

Diagram 10

14. Repeat with I and J, leaving outside edges of J unstitched.

15. Place stems and leaves; hand-stitch in place. Complete J appliqué.

16. Baste L pieces in place, inserting K in each one; stitch shapes in place to complete block appliqué.

17. Repeat to complete six blocks in each color combination.

Block Diagram 1
15" Square
Make 6

Block Diagram 2
15" Square
Make 6

ASSEMBLING THE TOP

Refer to the Assembly Diagram as needed for the following instructions.

1. Join the appliquéd blocks with A squares and the B and C triangles in diagonal rows; press (Diagram 11).

2. Join the rows to finish the quilt center; press seams in one direction.

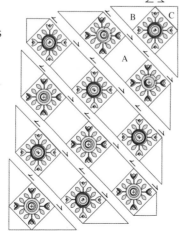

Diagram 11

PREPARING BORDER STRIPS

One border on the antique quilt is different than the rest. These instructions are given to make the quilt as shown. If you prefer to change the borders to make them all alike, prepare two F border strips with bud appliqué.

1. Prepare patterns for appliqué pieces as for block appliqué.

2. To make O circles, cut card-stock and fabric circles as marked on patterns. Sew a line of hand-basting stitches 1/8" from edge of fabric circle, knotting one end of the thread. Place a card-stock circle on the wrong side of the fabric and pull the thread to cinch the fabric around the circle (Diagram 12); press. Repeat for all circles.

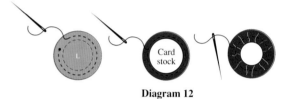

Diagram 12

3. Center and sew a circle to the top section of each N piece; cut a slit in the wrong side of each N piece under the circle and remove card-stock circles.

4. To make the top E strip, join six D and five DR pieces on the short ends, turn under seam allowance and arrange on one E strip with the edge of D 3/4" from the edge of E (Diagram 13). Baste pieces to hold in place. Trim end of last D piece even with E.

5. Insert a long and short orange-center N-O piece under D pieces (Diagram 14), placing only a short N-O piece under the last D piece. Repeat with red-center N-O pieces and the DR pieces. Baste and stitch all pieces in place.

6. Sew this appliquéd strip to the top of the quilt center; press seam toward E strip.

7. Repeat with five D and six DR pieces and N-O pieces on the remaining E strip to make the bottom strip referring to the Assembly Diagram for positioning of pieces.

8. Sew this appliquéd strip to the bottom of the quilt center; press seam toward E.

9. Create the appliquéd F strip as for E strips using eight each D and DR pieces. Sew this strip to the left side edge of the quilt center; press seam toward F.

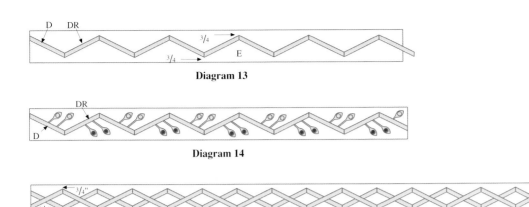

Diagram 13

Diagram 14

Diagram 15

10. To make the remaining side border strip, arrange 16 each D and DR pieces on the F strip, overlapping pieces as shown (Diagram 15). Stitch in place.

11. Sew the strip to the remaining side of the quilt center; press seam toward strip.

FINISHING THE QUILT

1. Piece backing to create a 80" x 101" rectangle.

2. Mark top for quilting, sandwich quilt layers, hand- or machine-quilt and bind edges referring to the General Quiltmaking Instructions. The quilt shown was hand-quilted in an echo design around appliqué shapes in blocks and borders and with the teardrop shape (given on page 33) in the background areas.

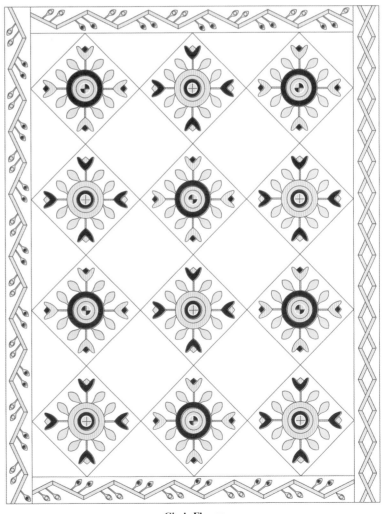

Circle Flower
Assembly Diagram 73³/₄" x 95"

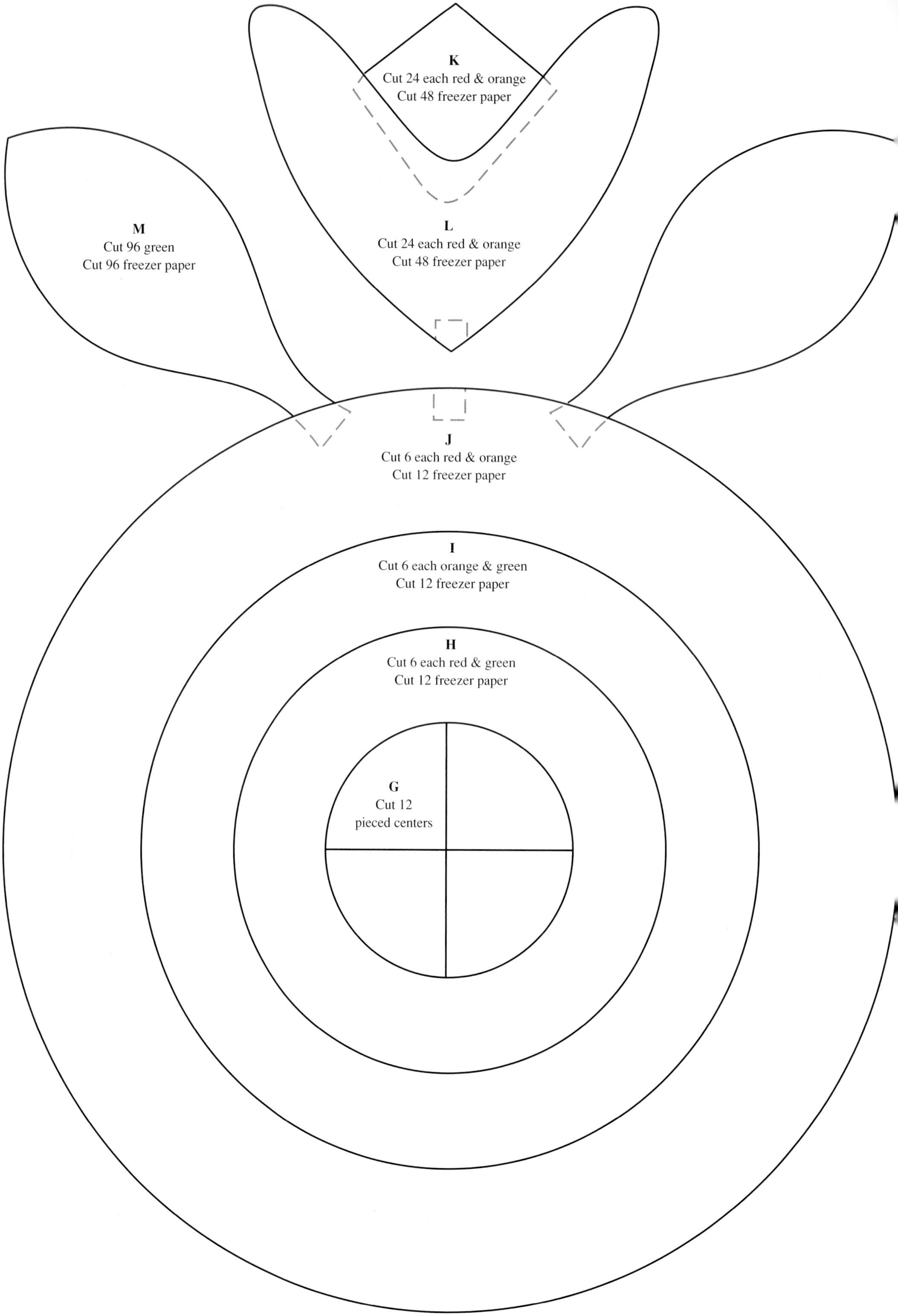

K
Cut 24 each red & orange
Cut 48 freezer paper

M
Cut 96 green
Cut 96 freezer paper

L
Cut 24 each red & orange
Cut 48 freezer paper

J
Cut 6 each red & orange
Cut 12 freezer paper

I
Cut 6 each orange & green
Cut 12 freezer paper

H
Cut 6 each red & green
Cut 12 freezer paper

G
Cut 12
pieced centers

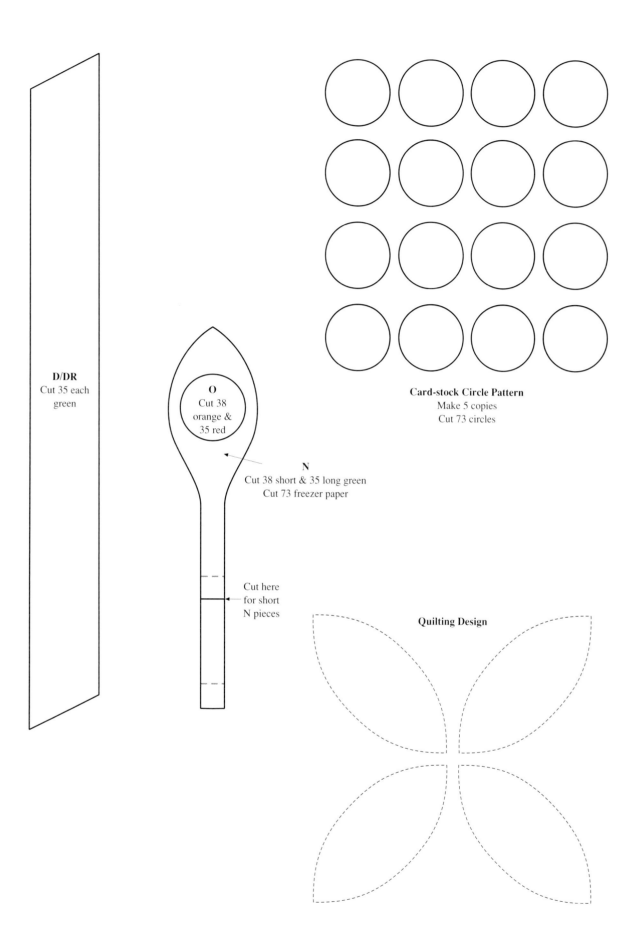

D/DR
Cut 35 each
green

O
Cut 38
orange &
35 red

N
Cut 38 short & 35 long green
Cut 73 freezer paper

Cut here
for short
N pieces

Card-stock Circle Pattern
Make 5 copies
Cut 73 circles

Quilting Design

Give It A Try...

If you don't like hand appliqué, try machine appliqué using fusible web to adhere pieces to the background. This method saves time. The fusible product does cause a stiffness in the appliquéd areas making it nearly impossible to hand-quilt inside of the fused areas. Hand-quilting all the background area is still an option. If you like this design but don't want to spend hours and hours doing handwork, give fusible appliqué a try on just one block to see how it works. You might want to purchase an appliqué pressing sheet as it facilitates accurate pattern placement.

- If making the sample to match the fabrics in your quilt, purchase extra of each fabric. If just making one block to give this pattern a try using fusible methods, check out your fabric stash to select fabrics. You will need 1/2 yard of background fabric for the center square and border pieces and 1/2 yard of the fabric taking the place of the fuchsia in the sample. Use fat quarters of the remaining fabrics (yellow mottled, green batik and large floral in the sample).

- Purchase 1/2 yard 18"-wide fusible web and 1/2 yard fabric stabilizer.

- Trace appliqué shapes for one block on the paper side of the fusible web, leaving a space between each shape.

- Cut out paper shapes, leaving a margin around each one. Fuse the shapes to the wrong side of the selected fabrics referring to the manufacturer's instructions.

- Cut out shapes on the marked lines; remove paper backing.

- Prepare a pieced G center using two 2" squares each of two fabrics, joining squares to make the G unit.

- Cut a 15 1/2" square background fabric; fold and crease to mark diagonal, vertical and horizontal centers.

- Trace the appliqué design onto a large piece of paper; place the appliqué pressing sheet over the pattern.

- Arrange the appliqué pieces on the pressing sheet in order as for quilt, using pattern beneath pressing sheet as a guide for placement. Fuse shapes in place as they are layered right on the sheet.

- When the complete motif has been formed and pressed, lift from the pressing sheet and place on the background square using creases as guides for placement of design. When satisfied with placement, fuse the entire motif in place.

- Cut a 15" square of fabric stabilizer; pin to the wrong side of the fused unit.

- Using thread to match fabrics, clear monofilament or variegated thread, machine-appliqué shapes in place using a narrow, close zigzag stitch.

- When appliqué stitching is complete, secure thread ends on the back side of the project; remove fabric stabilizer.

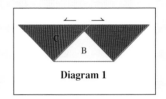

Diagram 1

- Cut one 8¼" square flower fabric; cut the square on both diagonals to make four A triangles.

- Cut two 5¼" squares light (yellow); cut each square on both diagonals to make eight B triangles.

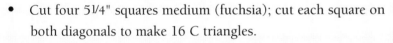

Diagram 2

- Cut four 5¼" squares medium (fuchsia); cut each square on both diagonals to make 16 C triangles.

- Cut eight 2" x 12" D rectangles background; fold and crease to mark the center.

- Sew a C triangle to each side of B (Diagram 1); press. Repeat for eight B-C units.

- Center and sew a B-C unit to D (Diagram 2); press. Repeat for eight B-C-D units.

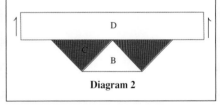

Diagram 3

- Using a rotary cutter and ruler, trim ends of D, extending angle of B-C units (Diagram 3).

- Sew a B-C-D unit to each side of A (Diagram 4); press.

- Sew a pieced unit to each side of the appliquéd center; stitch C pieces at corners and press.

- Add unpieced borders as desired to finish the top.

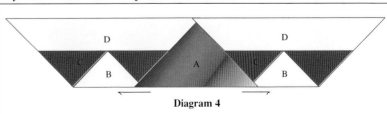

Diagram 4

Crossed T's

This Crossed T's quilt is a wonderful example of how sashing can be used to reduce the number of blocks needed to complete a bed-size quilt. (The Crossed T's block is shown in Figure 1, and the sashing in Figure 2.) The red prints used in the quilt date it to the mid-1800s. There is a question about why the maker mitered all the border strips in every corner except one. On that one corner, she butted the first strip only. It is barely noticeable on the quilt, but on close inspection it stands out.

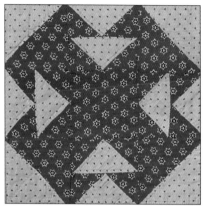

Figure 1

Binding a scalloped edge is not easy, but a narrow decorative binding combines with perfect stitching on this old quilt as shown in Figure 3. Hats off to the quiltmaker!

Figure 2

Check out Give It A Try to discover the differences between our instructions for making the sashing and the way it was made on the antique quilt. It is amazing how much time can be saved by adding a seam where there wasn't one before.

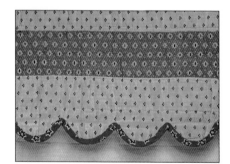

Figure 3

MAKE THE ANTIQUE QUILT

Finished Quilt Size 76" x 92½"
Finished Block Size 10½" Square
Number of Blocks 20

MATERIALS

Based on 42"-wide fabric.

Light red print ¾ yard

Red print 4½ yards

Cream print 4½ yards

Backing 5⅝ yards

Batting 82" x 98"

Coordinating thread

Rotary-cutting tools

Diagram 1

CUTTING INSTRUCTIONS

Refer to Diagram 1 to cut squares into triangles.
Light red print–fabric-width strips

- 9 strips 2¼" for O and P border strips

Red print–fabric-width strips

- 2 strips 4"; cut into twenty 4" A squares.

- 5 strips 4⅜"; cut into forty-six 4⅜" B squares and 2-1¾" x 11" F strips.

- 10 strips 2⅝"; cut into one-hundred-sixty 2⅝" squares. Cut squares on 1 diagonal to make 320 E triangles.

- 20 strips 1¾" for F

- 2 strips 5"; cut into twenty-four 2¼" I rectangles.

- 1 strip 10"; cut into twelve 2¼" J rectangles.

- 9 strips 2" for K and L borders

Red print

- Prepare 12 yards 1" wide bias binding

Cream print–fabric-width strips

- 5 strips 4⅜"; cut into forty 4⅜" C squares and one 4" x 11" G strip.

- 5 strips 5¼"; cut into forty 5¼" squares. Cut squares on both diagonals to make 160 D triangles.

- 10 strips 4" for G

- 2 strips 4¾"; cut into twelve 4¾" squares. Cut squares on both diagonals to make 48 H triangles.

- 9 strips 2¾" for M and N borders

- 9 strips 3" for Q and R borders

Use ¼" seam allowance for piecing. Arrows indicate pressing direction.

PIECING BLOCK UNITS

1. Draw a diagonal line from corner to corner on the wrong side of all C squares.

2. Place a B square right sides together with C; stitch ¼" on each side of the drawn line. Cut apart on the drawn line and press to complete one B-C unit (Diagram 2). Repeat for 80 B-C units.

Diagram 2

Diagram 3

3. Sew E to the short sides of D (Diagram 3); press. Repeat for 160 D-E units.

COMPLETING THE BLOCKS

1. Join two D-E units (Diagram 4); press.

2. Sew a B-C unit to each side of one D-E unit to make a side row (Diagram 5); press. Repeat.

Diagram 4

3. Sew a D-E unit to each side of A to make the center row (Diagram 6); press.

Diagram 5

4. Join the pieced rows to complete one block referring to the Block Diagram; press seams away from center row. Repeat for 20 blocks.

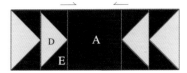

Diagram 6

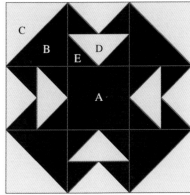

Block Diagram
10½" Square
Make 20

PIECING SASHING UNITS

1. Sew a fabric-width F strip to each side of a fabric-width G strip; press (Diagram 7). Repeat for 10 F-G strips.

2. Cut the F-G strips into (30) 11" F-G units (Diagram 7).

Diagram 7

3. Sew a 1¾" x 11" F strip to opposite sides of the 4" x 11" G strip to complete the remaining F-G unit; press seams toward F.

4. Join two H triangles with I (Diagram 8), matching one short edge of H triangles with one end of I; press. Excess I will extend at one end. Repeat for 24 H-I units. Fold and crease to mark the center of each unit on the I pieces (Diagram 9).

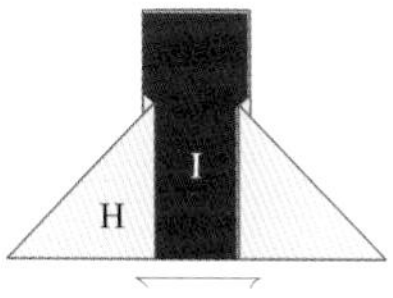

Diagram 8

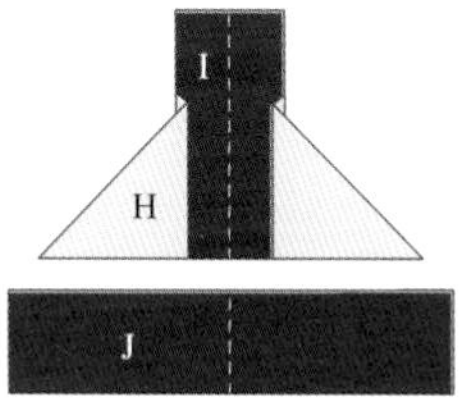

Diagram 9

5. Fold J rectangles to mark the center (Diagram 9). Center and sew an H-I unit to opposite sides of J (Diagram 10); press. Excess J will extend on both ends.

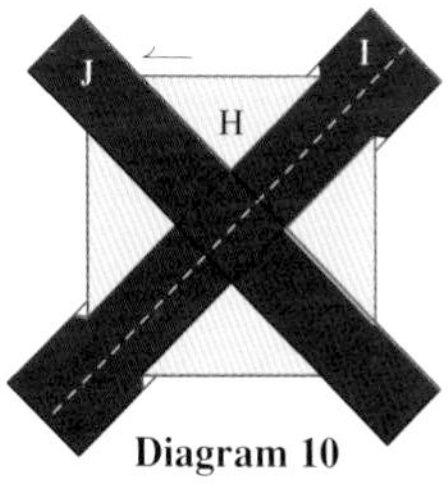

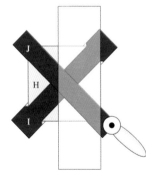

Diagram 10

6. Using a straightedge, trim excess I and J pieces even with H triangles to make 6½" H-I-J units (Diagram 11). Repeat for 12 units.

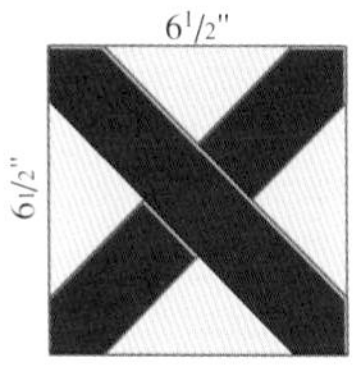

Diagram 11

ASSEMBLING THE TOP

Refer to the Assembly Diagram as needed for the following instructions.

1. Join four blocks with three F-G units to make a block row (Diagram 12); press. Repeat for five block rows.

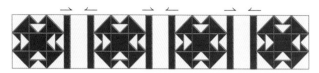

Diagram 12

2. Join four F-G units with three H-I-J units to make a sashing row (Diagram 13); press. Repeat for four sashing rows.

Diagram 13

3. Join the block rows with the sashing rows referring to the Assembly Diagram; press seams toward sashing rows.

4. Join the K-L border strips on short ends to make one long strip. Repeat with M-N, O-P and Q-R strips.

5. Join the border strips with right sides together in the following order: K-L to M-N to O-P to Q-R. Press seams toward darker fabric strips.

6. Cut two 80" and two 96" strips from the pieced strip.

7. Center and sew the 80" strips to the top and bottom and the 96" strips to opposite sides of the pieced center section, mitering corners (Diagram 14). Trim excess seam at mitered corners to ¼"; press seams open.

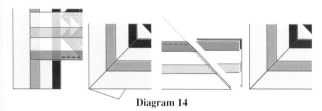

Diagram 14

8. Using the scallop pattern given on page 40, trace scallop design on outside edges of the quilt. Cut to make scalloped edge.

FINISHING THE QUILT

1. Piece backing to make an 82" x 98" rectangle.

2. Mark top for quilting, sandwich quilt layers, hand- or machine-quilt as desired and bind edges to finish referring to the General Quiltmaking Instructions. The quilt shown was hand-quilted using cream-colored quilting thread in the ditch of seams and through the center of each border strip.

3. Press under ¼" on both one long raw edge of the binding strip.

4. Leaving a 6" tail and starting on the curved part of one scallop, stitch the binding to the quilt edge, stretching binding at inside corners (Diagram 15); overlap binding at the beginning and end.

Diagram 15

5. Trim batting and backing even with scallop edge. Clip into seam between scallops (Diagram 16).

6. Turn binding to the back side of the quilt; hand-stitch in place, pleating binding between scallops as necessary.

Diagram 16

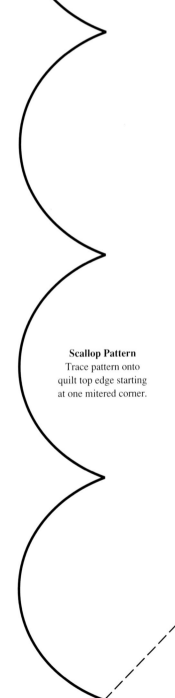

Scallop Pattern
Trace pattern onto
quilt top edge starting
at one mitered corner.

Crossed T's
Assembly Diagram 76" x 92½"

Give It A Try...

The blocks in the antique quilt could not be joined in rows because of the way the sashing squares and strips were pieced (Diagram 1). Instead the blocks are stitched

together with these units one at a time and joined in a
continuous process. This method makes it difficult to
organize the stitching for machine sewing. With the
simple addition of the triangles in the sashing squares
(Diagram 11 in Piecing Sashing Units on page 39),
piecing the top is much easier.

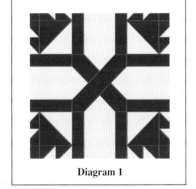

Diagram 1

The four-block sample shown uses a different fabric in the
triangles of the sashing squares than the wide G sash-
ing strip, giving it a different look. Four blocks, nine sashing squares and 12 sashing
strips are needed to create the sample shown. If you are thinking of trying the scallop edge, practice on your Give It A Try Sample.

*F*lower Basket

This pristine circa-1880s quilt is a testament to the striking use of vivid colors in fabrics so common to this time period. So often have these same colors faded through wear and cleaning to softer more subdued versions that we might be led to think that early quiltmakers preferred the

drabber colors. Compare the difference in the exact same blue dot and blue print used in this quilt (Figure 1 and close-up photo) and in Broken Star (page 9). The rich navy of this quilt has become the softer blue common to many surviving quilts of this era. So, too, do the green and red often change to much lighter colors and even to browns and tans. It is nice to know the quilter was able to use wonderful bright colors in her quilts to add sparkle to her hardworking life.

Figure 1

Flower Basket is also a fine example of quilting. A wonderful feathered branch was used in the sashing strips (Figure 2), clamshells fill the side and corner triangles and a large cable design surrounds the center in the border. The quilter even added a special touch with small quilted hearts and leaves on the outer edges of many of the sashing strips. All these designs were made in tiny, even hand stitches to create a beautiful bedcover (Figure 3).

Figure 2

Figure 3

MAKE THE ANTIQUE QUILT

Finished Quilt Size 90¼" Square
Finished Block Size 9" Square
Number of Blocks 25

MATERIALS

Based on 42" fabric width.

Chrome orange solid ½ yard

Red print ¾ yard

Green print ¾ yard

Navy dot ¾ yard

Navy print 3½ yards

Muslin 5¼ yards

Backing 8½ yards

Batting 96" square

Coordinating thread

Rotary-cutting tools

CUTTING INSTRUCTIONS

Refer to Diagram 1 for cutting squares into triangles.

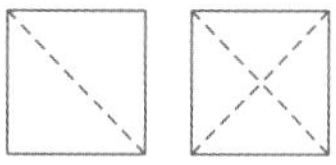

Diagram 1

There is no regular use of the different colors in the blocks in this antique quilt. Usually, the outer "flowers" in the basket are pieced of muslin and one color. The inside "flowers" use two other colors: three triangles of one color and six of the other. The basket is made of only one color. The cutting instructions below will create blocks to exactly match the quilt. If you wish to use a more planned use of color in your quilt, use the Block Diagram to determine placement and the number of each piece to cut from each color. Then refer to the size of each letter piece in the list below to plan your cutting. Keep in mind that every D, E and F square yields two triangles, so you will only cut half as many squares as you need of each color triangle.

Chrome orange solid–fabric-width strips

- 4 strips 2⅝"; cut into forty-four 2⅝" D squares and fifteen 2 5/8" E squares. Cut E squares on 1 diagonal to make 27 E triangles.

Red print–fabric-width strips

- 4 strips 2⅝"; cut into forty 2⅝" D squares and fourteen 2⅝" E squares. Cut E squares on 1 diagonal to make 30 E triangles.

- 1 strip 6⅛"; cut into five 6⅛" squares. Cut squares on 1 diagonal to make 9 F triangles.

- 1 strip 2⅞"; cut into nine 2⅞" squares. Cut squares on 1 diagonal to make 18 G triangles.

Green print–fabric-width strips

- 3 strips 2⅝"; cut into thirty-one 2⅝" D squares and six 2⅝" E squares. Cut E squares on 1 diagonal to make 12 E triangles.

- 1 strip 6⅛"; cut into four 6⅛" squares. Cut squares on 1 diagonal to make 8 F triangles.

- 1 strip 2⅞"; cut into eight 2⅞" squares. Cut squares on 1 diagonal to make 16 G triangles.

Navy dot–fabric-width strips

- 4 strips 2⅝"; cut into fifty-one 2⅝" D squares and three 2⅝" E squares. Cut E squares on 1 diagonal to make 6 E triangles.

- 1 strip 6⅛"; cut into four 6⅛" squares. Cut squares on 1 diagonal to make 8 F triangles.

- 1 strip 2⅞"; cut into eight 2⅞" squares. Cut squares on 1 diagonal to make 16 G triangles.

Navy print–fabric-width strips

- 32 strips 1⅜" for H

- 3 strips 4½"; cut into sixty-four 1¾" x 4½" K rectangles.

- 1 strip 9½"; cut into twenty-four 1¾" x 9½" L rectangles.

- 9 strips 5¼" for O and P borders

Muslin–fabric-width strips

- 6 strips 2⅝"; cut into eighty-eight 2⅝" A squares.

- 4 strips 5½"; cut into fifty 2½" x 5½" B rectangles.

- 2 strips 4⅞"; cut into thirteen 4⅞" squares. Cut squares on 1 diagonal to make 25 C triangles.

- 16 strips 4" for I

- 4 strips 4¾"; cut into thirty-two 4¾"

squares. Cut squares on both diagonals to make 128 J triangles.

- 1 strip 12¾"; cut into three 12¾" squares. Cut squares on both diagonals to make 12 M triangles.

- 1 strip 6⅝"; cut into two 6⅝" squares. Cut squares on 1 diagonal to make 4 N triangles.

- 10 strips 2¼" or 2½" for binding

Use ¼" seam allowance for piecing. Arrows indicate pressing direction.

PIECING THE BLOCK UNITS

1. Draw a diagonal line from corner to corner on the wrong side of each A square and 29 orange, 3 green and 7 navy D squares.

2. Place an A square right sides together with a red D square. Stitch ¼" from each side of the marked line; cut apart on the marked line and press toward the darker fabric to complete two red/muslin units (Diagram 2).

Diagram 2

3. Repeat step 2 to complete 250 units (Diagram 3), using the marked orange squares for the red/orange, green/orange and navy/orange units, the marked green squares for the red/green units and the marked navy squares for the red/navy and green/navy units. Set aside the extra units for another project.

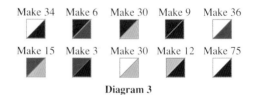

Diagram 3

4. Sew G to one end of B and press (Diagram 4). Repeat to make a B-G reversed unit using the same-color G and press (Diagram 4).

Diagram 4

5. Repeat step 4 to complete 25 B-G and B-G reversed unit pairs (Diagram 5).

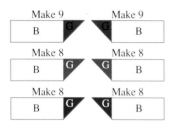

Diagram 5

COMPLETING THE BLOCKS

These instructions are given to piece the block shown in the Block Diagram. When complete, choose the pieces in colors to match each of the additional blocks in the quilt.

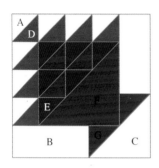

Block Diagram
9" Square
Make 25

1. Select seven green/muslin units, three red/navy units and three navy E triangles.

2. Arrange units in rows with E referring to Diagram 6.

Diagram 6

3. Join units in rows and press (Diagram 7).

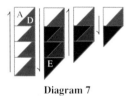

Diagram 7

4. Join the rows and press to complete the flower section (Diagram 8).

Diagram 8

5. Sew a red F triangle to the bottom of the flower section and press (Diagram 9).

Diagram 9

6. Sew a red B-G unit and B-G reversed unit to adjacent sides of the pieced section and press (Diagram 10).

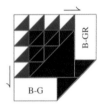

Diagram 10

7. Sew C to the bottom of the basket section to complete one block referring to the Block Diagram for positioning; press seam toward C.

8. Repeat to make 25 blocks.

ASSEMBLING THE TOP

Refer to the Assembly Diagram as needed for the following instructions.

1. Sew an H strip to opposite sides of I (Diagram 11); press. Repeat to make 16 pieced strips.

2. Cut the pieced strips into sixty-four 9 1/2" sashing strips (Diagram 11).

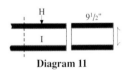

Diagram 11

3. Sew a J triangle to opposite sides of K and press (Diagram 12). Repeat for sixty-four J-K units.

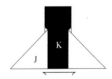

Diagram 12

4. Center and sew a J-K unit to opposite sides of L to make a sashing square, aligning the K pieces across the L strip (Diagram 13); press.

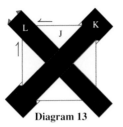

Diagram 13

5. Trim the K and L ends even with the edges of the J triangles to make a 5 3/4" sashing square (Diagram 14); repeat to make 24 sashing squares.

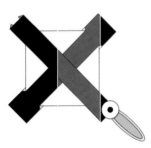

Diagram 14

6. Trim the K ends of the remaining J-K units even with the edges of J to make 16 sashing triangles (Diagram 15).

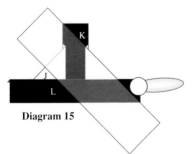

Diagram 15

7. Join blocks in diagonal rows with sashing strips and M and N triangles (Diagram 16); press seams toward sashing strips and triangles.

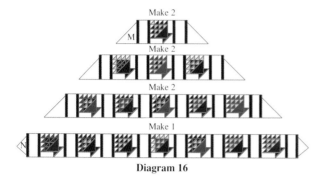

Diagram 16

8. Join sashing strips in rows with sashing squares and N triangles (Diagram 17); press seams toward sashing strips and N.

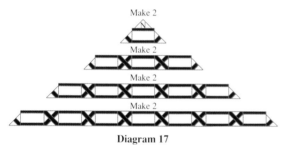

Diagram 17

9. Join the block rows with the sashing rows referring to the Assembly Diagram for positioning; press seams toward sashing rows.

10. Join the O/P strips on short ends to make a long strip; press seams in one direction. Cut into two 81¼" O strips and two 90¾" P strips.

11. Sew the O strips to opposite sides and the P strips to the remaining sides; press seams toward strips.

FINISHING

1. Piece backing to create a 96" square.

2. Mark top for quilting, sandwich quilt layers, hand- or machine-quilt and bind edges referring to the General Quiltmaking Instructions. Use the quilting design given in the I sashing strips. The quilter used a clamshell design in the N and M triangles in the antique quilt, but these small areas are the perfect place for using your favorite small quilting designs.

Flower Basket
Assembly Diagram 90¼" Square

Quilting
Design

Give It A Try...

Eliminate the Garden Maze sashing between the blocks, and instead lengthen it to use as a border treatment.

- Referring to quilt Cutting Instructions, cut 14 A squares, 8 B rectangles, 2 C squares, 2 J squares and four 4" x 18½" border strips from muslin. Cut 26 D squares, 6 E squares, 2 F squares and 4 G squares total from colored fabrics to yield four blocks. Cut four 1¾" x 4½" K strips, four 1⅛" x 9½" L strips and eight 1⅜" x 18½" border strips from navy print. Cut squares into triangles as directed.

- Complete four blocks referring to the Block Diagram, Piecing the Block Units and Completing the Blocks instructions on page 45. Join the blocks in two rows and join the rows to complete the center.

- Complete four J-K units referring to step 3 of Assembling the Top; center and sew an L strip to the long side of each J-K unit (Diagram 1); press.

- Trim L at an angle to match the J sides to complete a corner unit (Diagram 2).

- Sew a navy border strip to opposite long sides of each muslin border strip; press seams toward navy strips.

- Sew a border strip to opposite sides of the center; press seams toward strips.

- Sew a J-K unit to each end of the remaining border strips (Diagram 3); press.

- Sew a strip to the remaining sides of the center to complete the sample.

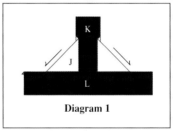

Diagram 1

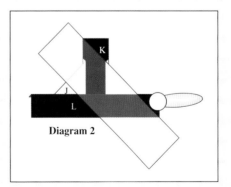

Diagram 2

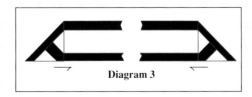

Diagram 3

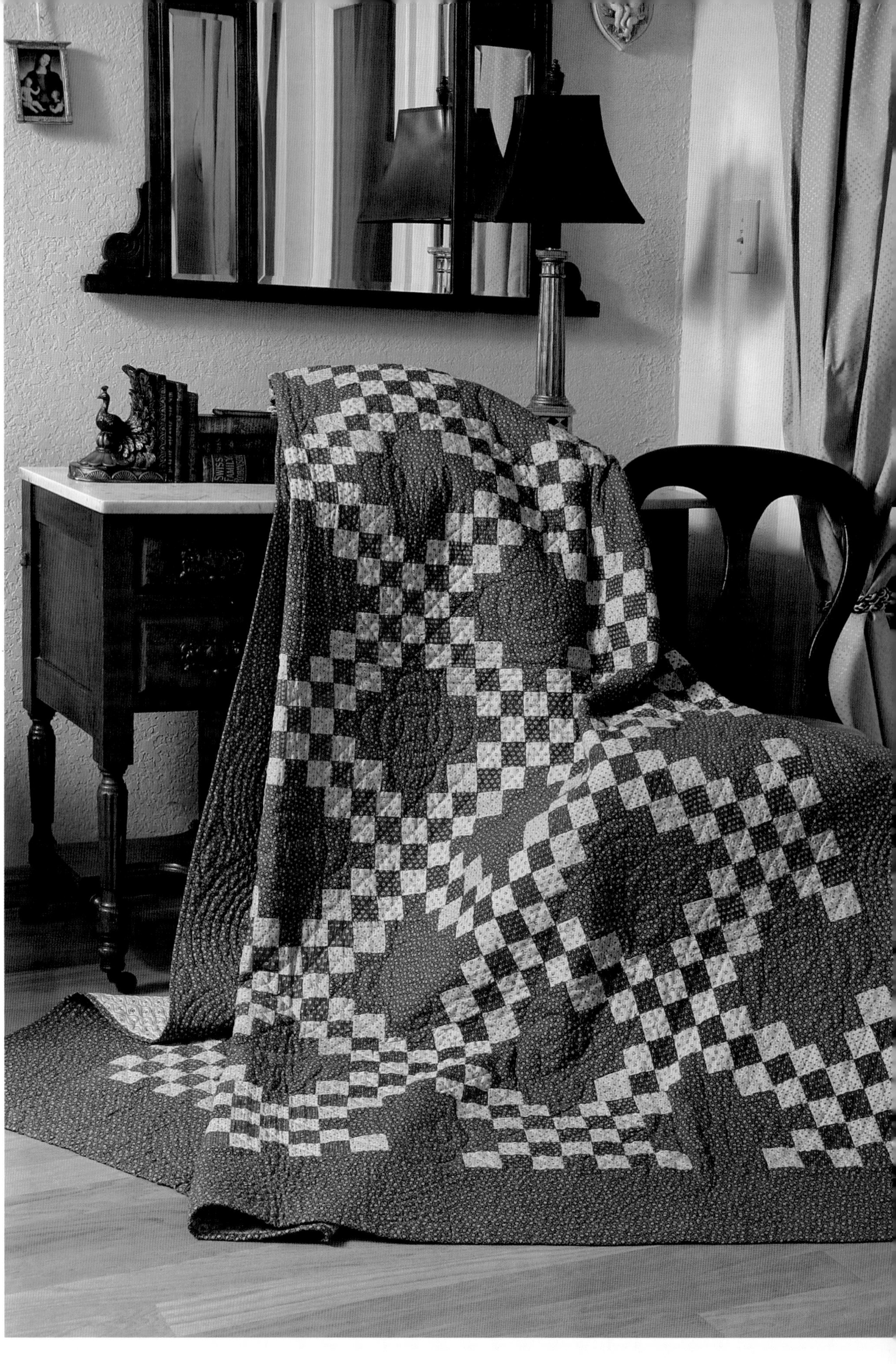

*I*rish Chain

The Irish Chain pattern is as familiar to quilters today as it was to quilters of the late 19th century. This quilt is a showcase of prints manufactured from 1830-1930 and popular with quilters of that entire period. The tiny green, yellow and red calicoes can be found in planned designs and scrap quilts alike. This quiltmaker used her supply of these fabrics to create a much different version of an Irish Chain. It is usually seen with colored "chains" on a white or light background. The maker of this example used her skills with color to make the bright yellow and red of her chains seem to jump out from the receding green background (Figure 1). She created a quilt of great depth and dimension.

Figure 1

This quilt contains another unusual feature: the yellow squares at the corners of the green open area are appliquéd in place instead of pieced with strips of green. This allowed the early quiltmaker to show off her handstitching skills (Figure 2). It gives today's quilter a chance to use some of the many decorative machine stitches to hold these squares in place.

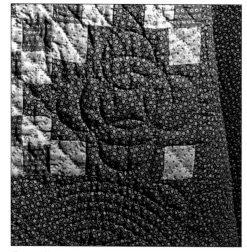
Figure 2

MAKE THE ANTIQUE QUILT

Finished Quilt Size 92¾" x 101½"
Finished Block Size 8¾" Square
Number of Blocks 90

MATERIALS

Based on 42" fabric width.

Red print 1¾ yards

Yellow print 3⅛ yards

Green print 6⅞ yards

Backing 9¼ yards

Batting 99" x 108"

Coordinating thread

Rotary-cutting tools

Optional Supplies

    Machine-embroidery thread or clear monofilament

    2 yards 18"-wide fusible web

    1¾ yards 20"-wide fabric stabilizer

    Heat-resistant template material

    Spray starch and small brush

CUTTING INSTRUCTIONS

Red print–fabric-width strips

- 23 strips 2¼" for C

Yellow print–fabric-width strips

- 12 strips 2½"; cut into one-hundred-eighty 2½" B squares for hand or invisible-machine appliqué; or, 10 B strips 2¾" for fusible appliqué (see Give It A Try before cutting B pieces).

- 31 strips 2¼" for D

Green print–fabric-width strips

- 12 strips 9¼"; cut into forty-five 9¼" A squares.

- 11 strips 2¼" for E

- 10 strips 7½" for F and G borders

- 10 strips 2¼" or 2½" for binding

Fusible web *(for use in fusible appliqué only)*

- 26 strips 2½" x 18"

Fabric stabilizer *(for use in invisible-machine and fusible appliqué only)*

- 23 strips 2½" x 20"; cut into one-hundred-eighty 2½" squares.

Use ¼" seam allowance for piecing. Arrows indicate pressing direction.

PIECING BLOCK I

1. Join one E strip and two each C and D strips to make an X pieced strip (Diagram 1); press. Repeat to make five pieced strips.

2. Join two C and three D strips to make a Y pieced strip (Diagram 2); press. Repeat to make five pieced strips.

Diagram 1

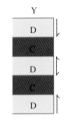

Diagram 2

3. Join one C strip and two each D and E strips to make a Z pieced strip (Diagram 3); press. Repeat to make three pieced strips.

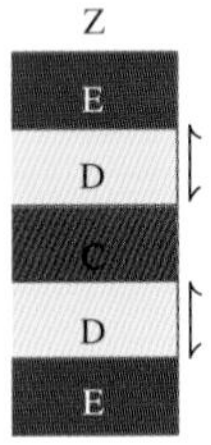

4. Cut the pieced strips into 2¼" segments to make 90 X, 90 Y and 45 Z rows (Diagram 4).

Diagram 3

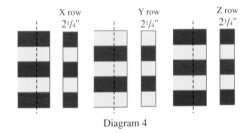

Diagram 4

5. Join one Z row and two each X and Y rows to complete one block referring to Block Diagram 1; press seams in one direction. Repeat to make 45 blocks.

COMPLETING BLOCK 2

1. Prepare 180 B pieces and stitch in place on each corner of A to complete one block referring to Give It A Try; repeat to make 45 blocks.

ASSEMBLING THE TOP

Refer to the Assembly Diagram as needed for the following instructions.

1. Join blocks to make two different block rows (Diagram 5); press. Repeat to make five of each row.

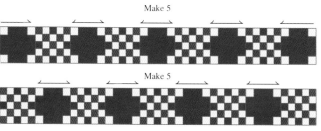

Make 5

Make 5

Diagram 5

2. Join the rows to complete the top referring to the Assembly Diagram for positioning of rows; press seams in one direction.

3. Join the F/G strips on short ends with a diagonal seam to make a long strip; trim seams to 1/4" and press seams in one direction. Cut into two 79 1/4" F strips and two 102" G strips.

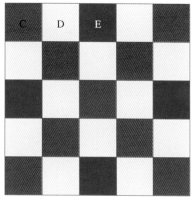

Block Diagram 1
8 3/4" Square
Make 45

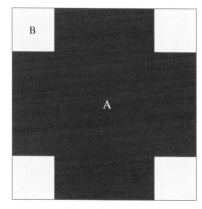

Block Diagram 2
8 3/4" Square
Make 45

4. Sew an F strip to opposite short ends of the center; press seams toward F.

5. Sew a G strip to opposite long sides of the center; press seams toward G.

FINISHING

1. Piece backing to create a 99" x 108" rectangle.

2. Mark top for quilting, sandwich quilt layers, hand- or machine-quilt and bind edges referring to the General Quiltmaking Instructions. Use the quilting design given in the A squares to duplicate the antique quilt.

Irish Chain
Assembly Diagram 92 3/4" x 101 1/2"

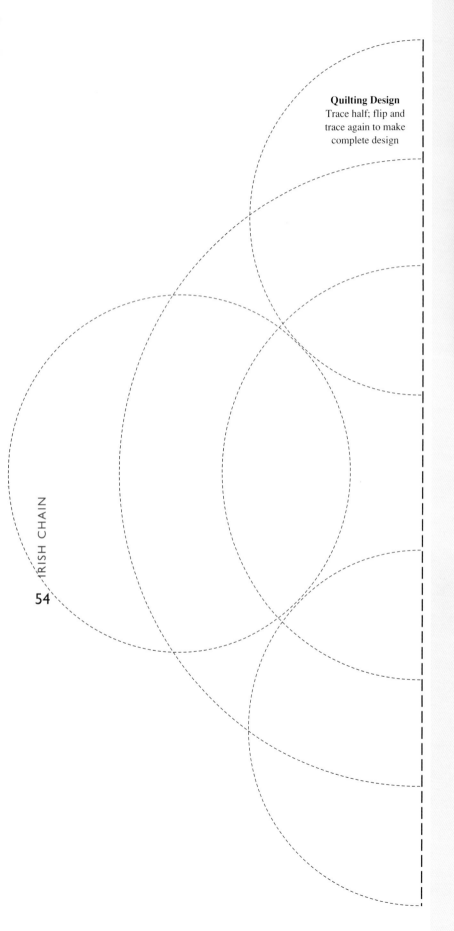

Quilting Design
Trace half; flip and
trace again to make
complete design

*G*ive It A Try...

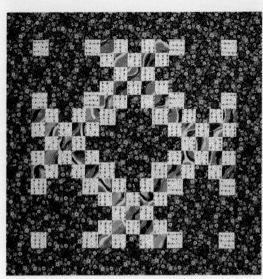

The corner B squares of Block 2 were hand-appliquéd on the antique quilt. Choose your favorite method of appliqué to prepare and stitch the B squares on your quilt.

HAND OR INVISIBLE-MACHINE APPLIQUÉ

- Cut 2¹/2" B squares as directed in the Cutting Instructions.

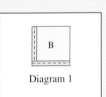

B

Diagram 1

- Turn under two adjacent edges of each square ¹/4" and baste to hold (Diagram 1).

- Or, cut a 2¼"-square heat-resistant template; place on the wrong side of a B square (Diagram 2). Brush the exposed seam allowances with spray starch and press allowances over edge of template with dry iron (Diagram 3). Repeat with all B squares, replacing the template as edges become distorted.

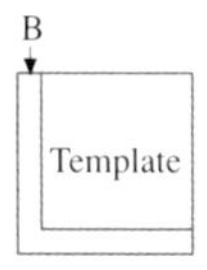

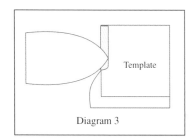

Diagram 2

- Place B on each corner of an A square, aligning raw edges; pin to hold.

- Hand-stitch turned-under edges in place using thread to match B; remove basting.

- Or, place a square of fabric stabilizer under B on the wrong side of A; machine-stitch in place along the turned-under edges using clear monofilament or thread to match B and a machine blind stitch (Diagram 4). Remove stabilizer.

Diagram 3

FUSIBLE APPLIQUÉ

- Bond the fusible web strips to the wrong side of the B fabric strips, butting the end of one fusible strip against the next to cover the entire fabric strip length and placing the edge of the fusible very close to the edge of the fabric strip (Diagram 5); trim excess fusible for use on another strip.

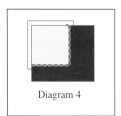

Diagram 4

- Straighten one long edge of the fused strips to place fabric and fusible evenly along edge (Diagram 6); cut one 2¼" strip from each fused strip.

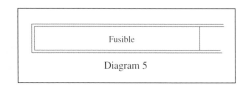

Diagram 5

- Remove the paper backing to make it easier to work with the strips. Be very careful not to get the fusible near an iron at this stage. Do not remove the paper if using double-stick fusible web.

- Cut the fused strips into one-hundred-eighty 2¼" B squares.

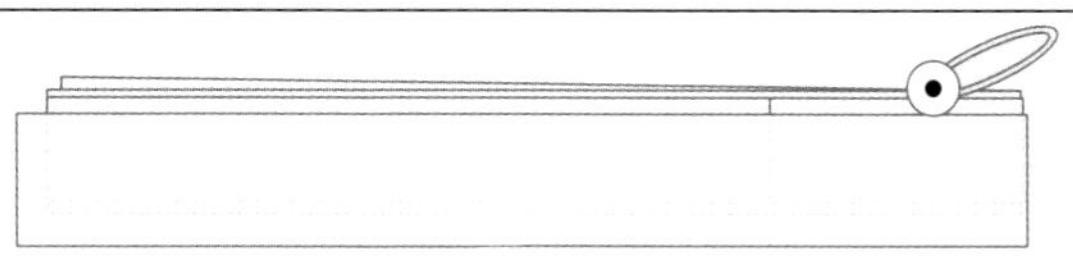

Diagram 6

- Place a B square on each corner of A, matching corners of A and B; fuse squares in place according to manufacturer's instructions.

- Place a square of fabric stabilizer under B on the wrong side of A; machine-stitch in place along the two inner edges of B using a decorative machine stitch and thread of choice (Diagram 7). Remove stabilizer.

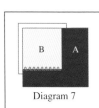

Diagram 7

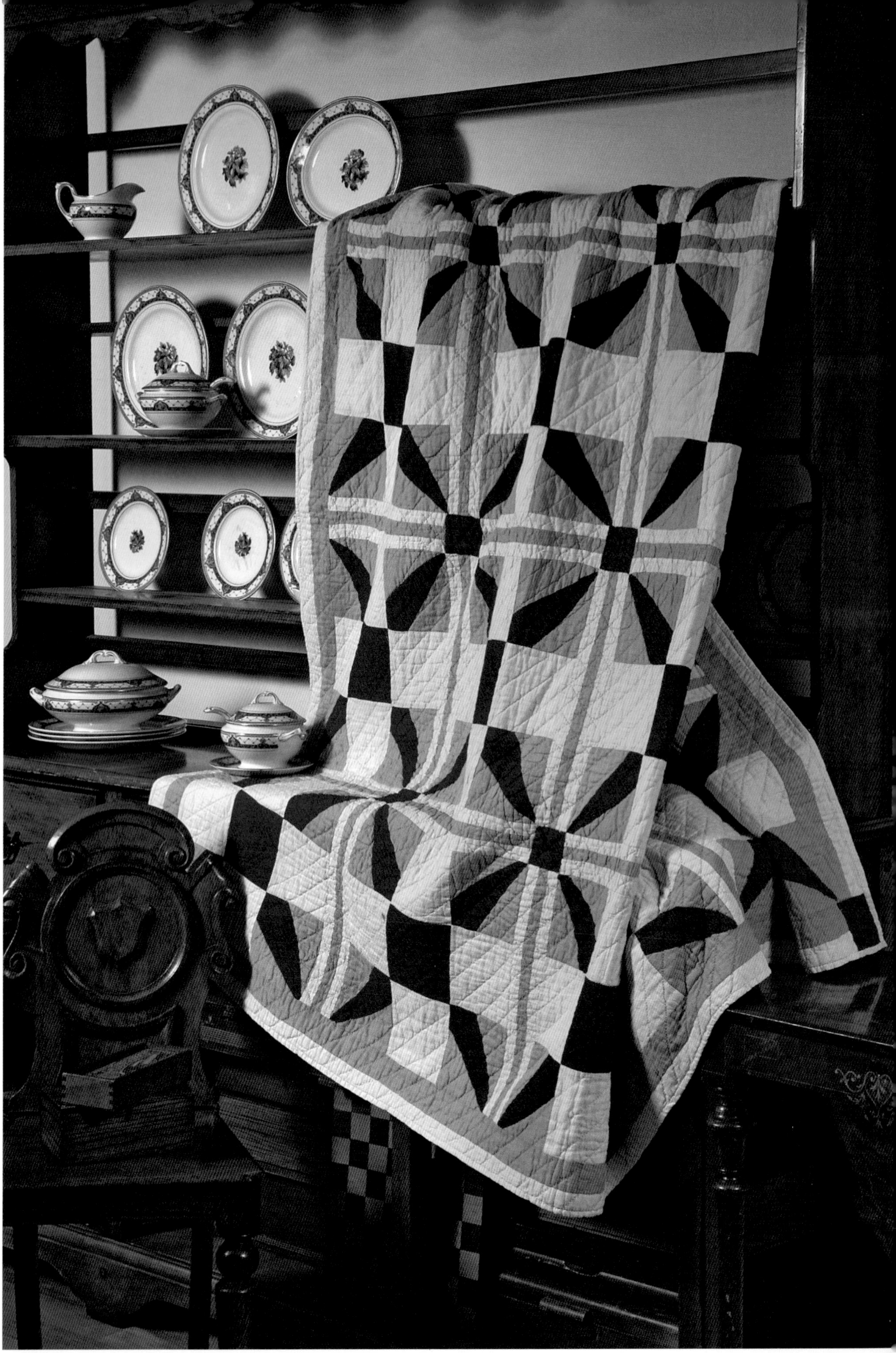

King David's Crown

At first glance, it is difficult to pick out the block from the sashing in the creative setting of this late-19th century quilt. Is it a Nine-Patch block with a small red square in the middle and striped side units as in Figure 1, or is it a Nine-Patch block with a large red center square and plain side units as in Figure 2? A closer look reveals the last to be true with sashing that makes the deceptive secondary design.

The fabrics in this quilt are good examples of the permanence of Turkey red used in much of the 1800s and the impermanence of green dyes used in this same period. Throughout this century, green was created by dyeing first in blue and then in yellow or vice versa. One or another of these colors often bled out leaving a green with either a bluish cast, a bright yellow-green look or a brownish-green shade. This quilt shows a green that looks overall like a light olive green but in places has blue smudges that attest to its origin.

Figure 1

Figure 2

MAKE THE ANTIQUE QUILT

Finished Quilt Size 67¼" x 83"
Finished Block Size 13½" Square
Number of Blocks 20

MATERIALS

Based on 42" fabric width.

Red solid 1¾ yards*

Light olive solid 2¼ yards*

Muslin 3½ yards

Backing 5¼ yards

Batting 73" x 89"

Coordinating thread

Template material

Rotary-cutting tools

See Give It A Try for possible yardage changes.

CUTTING INSTRUCTIONS

Red solid–fabric-width strips

- 3 strips 5" for A
- 5 strips 7" for C, or 10 strips 5" for C (see Give It A Try)
- 1 strip 2¾"; cut into twelve 2¾" H squares.

Red solid

- Four 3¾" M squares

Light olive solid–fabric-width strips

- 8 strips 5⅛" for D and DR, or 8 strips 6" for D and DR (see Give It A Try).
- 11 strips 1¼" for G
- 7 strips 2¼" for I and K borders

Muslin–fabric-width strips

- 6 strips 5" for B
- 5 strips 5"; cut into forty 5" E squares.
- 22 strips 1¼" for F
- 7 strips 2" for J and L borders
- 8 strips 2¼" or 2½" for binding

Use ¼" seam allowance for piecing. Arrows indicate pressing direction.

PIECING THE BLOCKS

1. Prepare templates for C and D pieces on page 60.

2. Unfold and press C strips; layer right sides up. Place the C template on the layered strip and cut pieces along length to total 80 C pieces, turning template end to end from piece to piece (Diagram 1).

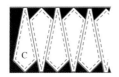

Diagram 1

3. Unfold, press and layer four D strips with right sides up. Use D template to cut 80 D pieces total along length through all layers (Diagram 2); be sure to cut angled corner to help align pieces for stitching.

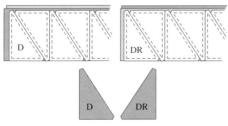

Diagram 2

4. Unfold, press and layer four D strips with wrong sides up. Use D template to cut 80 DR pieces total along length (Diagram 2); be sure to cut angled corner to help align pieces for stitching.

5. Sew D and DR pieces to opposite long sides of C, aligning angled corner of D piece with short edge of C (Diagram 3); press. Repeat for 80 C-D units.

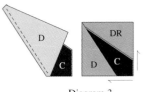

Diagram 3

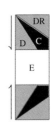

Diagram 4

6. Sew a C-D unit to opposite sides of an E square and press to complete a side row (Diagram 4). Repeat for 40 side rows.

7. Sew an A strip between two B strips (Diagram 5); press. Repeat to make three pieced strips.

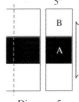

Diagram 5

8. Cut the pieced strips into twenty 5" segments to make center rows (Diagram 5).

9. Sew a center row between two side rows to complete one block referring to the Block Diagram for positioning; press seams toward the center row. Repeat to make 20 blocks.

ASSEMBLING THE TOP

Refer to the Assembly Diagram as needed for the following instructions.

1. Sew a G strip between two F strips (Diagram 6); press. Repeat to make 11 pieced strips.

2. Cut the pieced strips into thirty-one 14" sashing strips (Diagram 6).

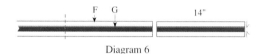

Diagram 6

3. Join four blocks with three sashing strips to make a block row; press seams toward sashing strips. Repeat to make five block rows.

4. Join four sashing strips with three H squares to make a sashing row; press seams toward sashing strips. Repeat to make four sashing rows.

5. Join the block rows with the sashing rows referring to the Assembly Diagram for positioning of rows; press seams toward sashing rows.

6. Join the I/K strips on short ends to make a long strip; press seams in one direction. Cut into two 77" I strips and two 61¼" K strips.

7. Join the J/L strips on short ends to make a long strip; press seams in one direction. Cut into two 77" J strips and two 61¼" L strips.

8. Sew an I strip to a J strip; press seam toward J. Repeat to make two I/J strips. Repeat with K and L strips to make two K/L strips.

9. Sew an I/J strip to opposite long sides of the center; press seams toward strips.

10. Sew an M square to each end of the K/L strips; press seams toward K/L.

11. Sew the pieced strips to the top and bottom of the center; press seams toward strips.

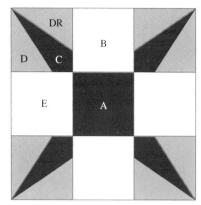

Block Diagram
13½" Square
Make 20

FINISHING

1. Piece backing to create a 73" x 89" rectangle.

2. Mark top for quilting, sandwich quilt layers, hand- or machine-quilt and bind edges referring to the General Quiltmaking Instructions.

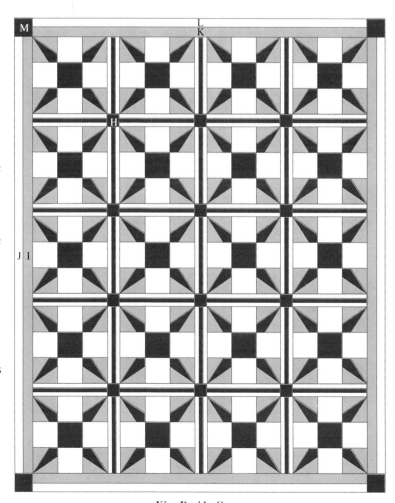

King David s Crown
Assembly Diagram 67¼" x 83"

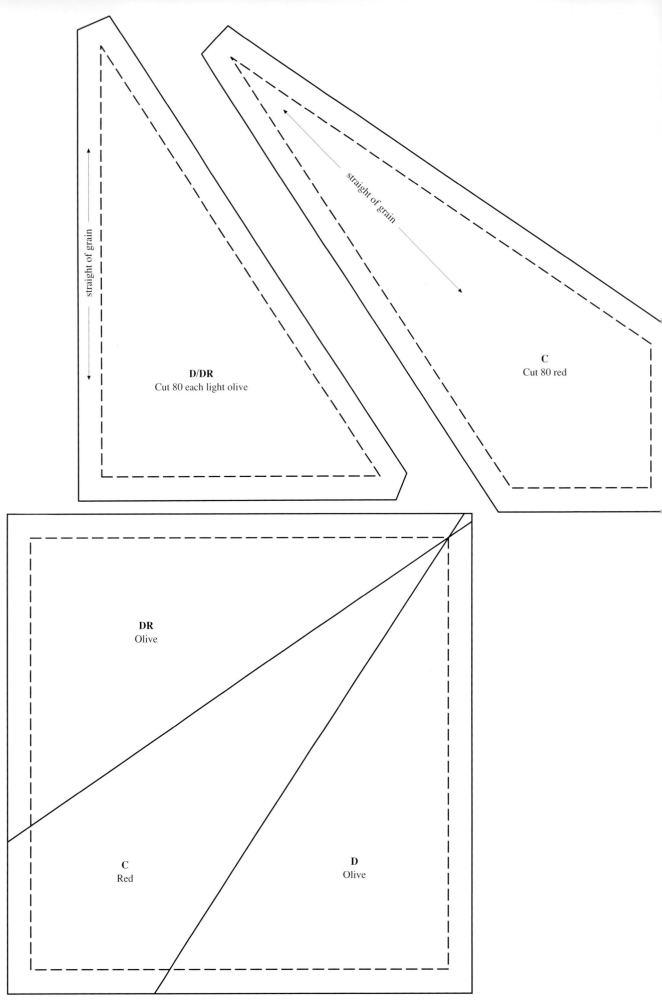

straight of grain

D/DR
Cut 80 each light olive

straight of grain

C
Cut 80 red

DR
Olive

C
Red

D
Olive

C-D Paper-Piecing Pattern
Make 80 copies

Give It A Try...

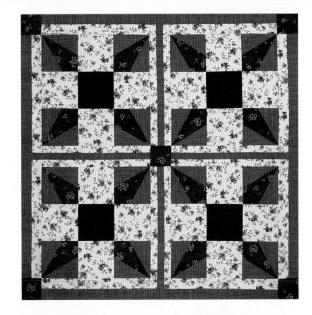

Create sharp points on the C pieces every
time with the precision of paper piecing.

- Purchase 2⅛ yards red solid and 2⅜ yards
  light olive solid to paper-piece the C-D
  units, instead of the yardage listed in the
  materials list.

- Cut the 5" C strips into eighty 5" C squares.

- Cut the 6" D/DR strips into eighty 4" x 6"
  rectangles; cut each rectangle on one diagonal to
  make 80 each D and DR pieces (Diagram 1).

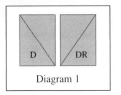

Diagram 1

- Photocopy 80 C-D Paper-Piecing Patterns.

- Pin a C square on the unmarked side of one
  pattern being sure that the square exactly covers
  the whole C-D square area (Diagram 2).

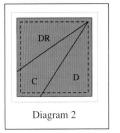

Diagram 2

- Place a D piece right sides together on the C
  square, extending the edge of D ¼" into the D
  section of the pattern (Diagram 3); pin to hold.

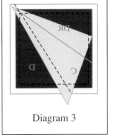

Diagram 3

- Change stitch length to 20 stitches per inch.
  Flip the pattern over to the printed side and
  stitch along the line between the C and D sections, stitching to the
  outside edges of the pattern (Diagram 4).

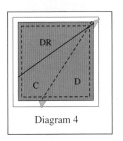

Diagram 4

- Fold the D piece over and check that it covers the D section
  (including seam allowances). If so, trim C-D seam allowance to
  ¼" (Diagram 5); press D to the right side. If the D piece does not
  cover the D section, remove piece, re-align and stitch again. If
  aligning pieces is difficult, machine-baste pieces, check for
  alignment and then stitch in place with the shorter stitch length.

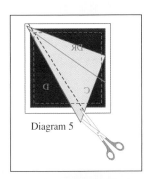

Diagram 5

- Repeat with a DR piece on the other edge of C (Diagram 6).

- Trim fabric and paper edges even with outer solid line of pattern
  all around to complete one C-D unit. Repeat to make 80 C-D
  units.

- Remove the paper backing from the C-D units after the units have
  been stitched into the blocks.

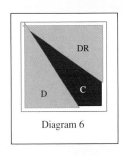

Diagram 6

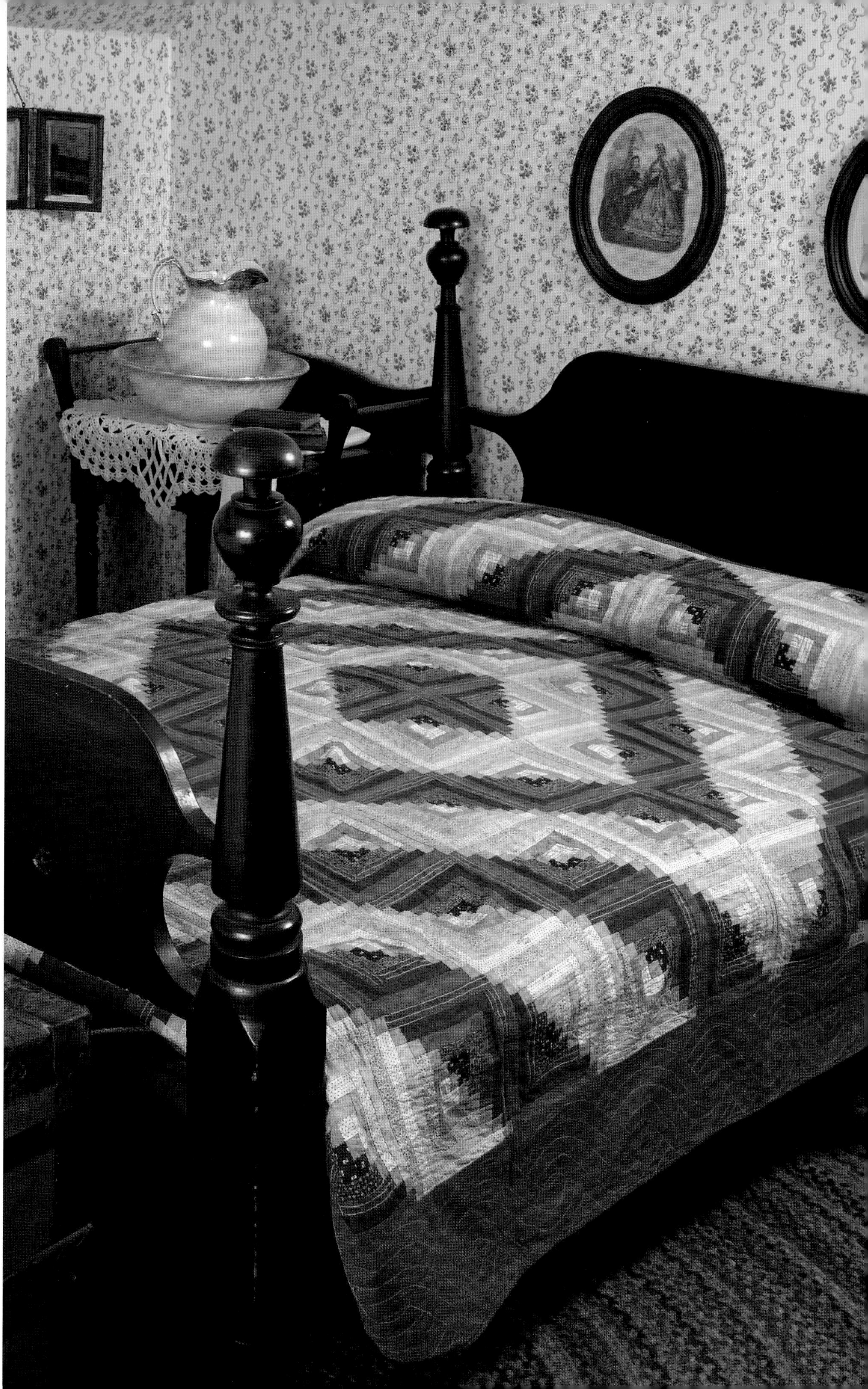

*L*og Cabin Trails

The logs in this circa 1860s Log Cabin Trails quilt finish at ¾". This requires many strips to create
a block of any size. What is especially charming about
this quilt is the small gold square that creates the trail
in the quilt's design (Figure 1). As the sample was being
planned, it was apparent that the original quiltmaker
had design talents. She had the foresight to realize that
if the outer-edge strips of the blocks were repeated on
every square, a large area of one fabric would dominate
the quilt top. To avoid this, she alternated the positioning of the fabrics to create two different blocks.

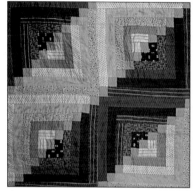

Figure 1

Another curious thing about this quilt is that yardage
was used instead of scraps. Most Log Cabin-design
quilts from the 19th century were made using scraps
because such narrow pieces could be used and even
joined to make strips of the required size. This quiltmaker apparently could afford the luxury of purchasing fabric yardage for her quilt.

Another mystery is why there is no batting inside. Most quilts
were made to be used as bedcovers for warmth. This
quilt was obviously used in warmer weather. When
examining the quilt to see how it was constructed, it was
determined that the strips were stitched to the wrong
side of a backing square and then joined by hand using
invisible seams. The borders were added and a treadle

Figure 2

machine was used to stitch the cable design in the borders to hold them together (Figure 2).
Many of the early Log Cabin quilts were without borders, but this quilt would not have fit a
larger bed without them.

MAKE THE ANTIQUE QUILT

Finished Quilt Size 79" x 95½"
Finished Block Size 8¼" Square
Number of Blocks 80

MATERIALS

Based on 42" fabric width.

White-with-black stripe ⅜ yard

Brown-and-white print ⅜ yard

Brown-and-white texture ⅝ yard

Pink solid ⅝ yard

Soldier blue solid 1⅛ yards

Cream solid 1⅛ yards

Gold solid 1½ yards

Brown-with-white stripe 1½ yards

White-with-black dots 1½ yards

White print 1½ yards

Brown solid 4¼ yards

Backing 5⅝ yards

Batting (not in original) 85" x 101"

Coordinating thread

Rotary-cutting tools

CUTTING INSTRUCTIONS

Be careful to label each set of pieces when cutting so as not to get them confused during the stitching process.

Gold solid–fabric-width strips

- 37 strips 1¼" for A

Brown-and-white print–fabric-width strips

- 3 strips 1¼" for B
- 3 strips 2" for D

White-with-black stripe–fabric-width strips

- 3 strips 1¼" for C
- 3 strips 2" for E

Brown-and-white texture–fabric-width strips

- 3 strips 23/4"; cut into eighty 11/4" rectangles for F.
- 3 strips 31/2"; cut into eighty 11/4" rectangles for G.

Pink solid–fabric-width strips

- 3 strips 2¾" for H
- 3 strips 3½" for I

Brown-with-white stripe–fabric-width strips

- 2 strips 4¼"; cut into forty 1¼" rectangles for J1.
- 2 strips 5"; cut into forty 1¼" rectangles for K1.
- 2 strips 7¼"; cut into forty 1¼" rectangles for R2.
- 2 strips 8"; cut into forty 1¼" rectangles for S2.

White-with-black dots–fabric-width strips

- 2 strips 4¼" for L1
- 2 strips 5" for M1
- 2 strips 7¼" for T2
- 2 strips 8" for U2

Soldier blue solid–fabric-width strips

- 3 strips 5¾"; cut into eighty 1¼" rectangles for N.
- 3 strips 6½"; cut into eighty 1¼" rectangles for N.

Cream solid–fabric-width strips

- 3 strips 5¾" for P
- 3 strips 6½" for Q

Brown solid–fabric-width strips

- 2 strips 4¼"; cut into forty 1¼" rectangles for J2.
- 2 strips 5"; cut into forty 1¼" rectangles for piece K2.
- 2 strips 7¼"; cut into forty 1¼" rectangles for piece R1.
- 2 strips 8"; cut into forty 1¼" rectangles for piece S1.

Brown solid–along remaining length of fabric

- 2 strips 7" x 66½" for V borders
- 2 strips 7" x 96" for W borders
- 4 strips 2¼" or 2½" for binding

White print–fabric-width strips

- 2 strips 4¼" for L2
- 2 strips 5" for M2
- 2 strips 7¼" for T1
- 2 strips 8" for U1

Use 1/4" seam allowance for piecing. Arrows indicate pressing direction.

PIECING THE BLOCKS

1. Join an A strip with a B and C strip with right sides together along length; press. Repeat for three pieced strips; cut pieced strips into eighty 1¼" A-B-C segments (Diagram 1).

Diagram 1

2. Sew an A strip to a D strip with right sides together along length; press. Repeat for three pieced strips; cut pieced strips into eighty 1¼" A-D segments (Diagram 2).

Diagram 2

3. Sew an A strip to an E strip with right sides together along length; press. Repeat for three pieced strips; cut pieced strips into eighty 1¼" A-E segments (Diagram 3).

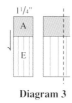
Diagram 3

4. Sew an A strip with right sides together along the length to each of the remaining light-colored strips; press. Cut each H, I, P and Q pieced strips into eighty 1¼" segments and remaining pieced strips into forty 1¼" segments.

5. Referring to Diagram 4, join an A-B-C segment with one each A-D and A-E segments and press to complete a block center. Repeat for 80 block centers.

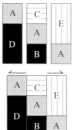
Diagram 4

6. Add F to the A-B-D side of a block center and press (Diagram 5). Repeat for all block centers.

Diagram 5

7. Add G to the A-D side of the block center and press (Diagram 6). Repeat for all block centers.

Diagram 6

8. Add an A-H segment to the A-C-E side of the block center and press (Diagram 7). Repeat for all block centers.

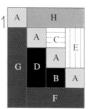
Diagram 7

9. Add an A-I segment to the remaining side of the pieced center and press (Diagram 8). Repeat for all block centers.

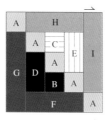
Diagram 8

10. Continue adding pieces around the center referring to the Block Diagrams to complete 40 each blocks 1 and 2; press seams toward the segment just added. *The white-with-black-dots and the white print switch positions with the brown solid and the brown-with-white stripe from Block 1 to Block 2. This change prevents butting*

of same-fabric strips when blocks are joined.

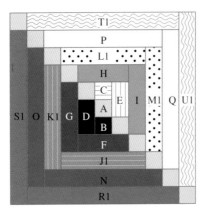

Block Diagram 1
8¹/4" Square
Make 40

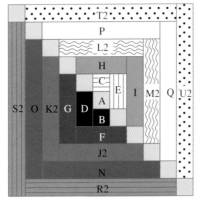

Block Diagram 2
8¹/4" Square
Make 40

ASSEMBLING THE TOP

1. Join the blocks in two different rows of eight blocks each (Diagram 9); press. Alternate Blocks 1 and 2 to keep outside fabric strips of the same fabric from coming together.

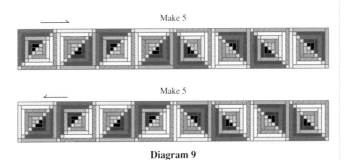

Make 5

Make 5

Diagram 9

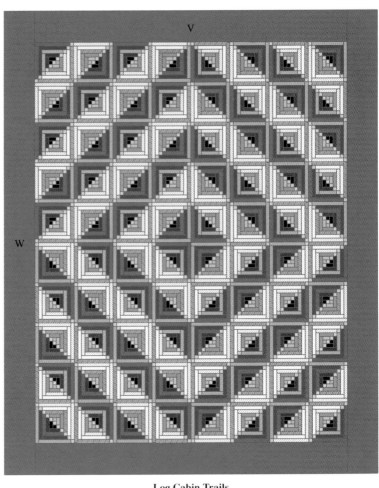

Log Cabin Trails
Assembly Diagram 79" x 95¹/2"

2. Join the rows to complete the Barn-Raising design in the quilt center referring to the Assembly Diagram for positioning of rows; press seams in one direction.

3. Sew V border strips to the top and bottom and W border strips to opposite sides of the quilt center; press seams toward V and W strips.

FINISHING THE QUILT

1. Piece backing to create an 85" x 101" rectangle.

2. Mark top for quilting, sandwich quilt layers, hand- or machine-quilt and bind edges referring to the General Quiltmaking Instructions. *The quilt shown did not have a batting and was hand-stitched in the ditch of seams to the backing. The borders were machine-stitched in an uneven cable design.*

*G*ive It A Try...

To help you find the rhythm needed to complete a quilt with repetitive stitching such as Log Cabin Trails, stitch a four-block sample like the one shown. Blue fabrics are used for the dark side, while cream fabrics are used on the light side. Red is used to create the trail in the blocks.

- Create two each blocks 1 and 2 referring to the instructions for Piecing the Blocks on page 65 for the quilt, cutting only four of each piece/segment listed. To make strip piecing easy, cut 6"-8" rectangles in the lengths listed for each piece for the quilt. For example, for piece F, cut one 2¾" x 6"-8" rectangle dark fabric. Then cut the rectangle into 1¼" segments.

- For the A-B-C units, cut a 1¼" by 6"-8" strip each dark (B), red (A) and light (C). Join the strips and cut into 1¼" A-B-C segments.

- Create blocks referring to quilt instructions and join.

- Add borders as desired.

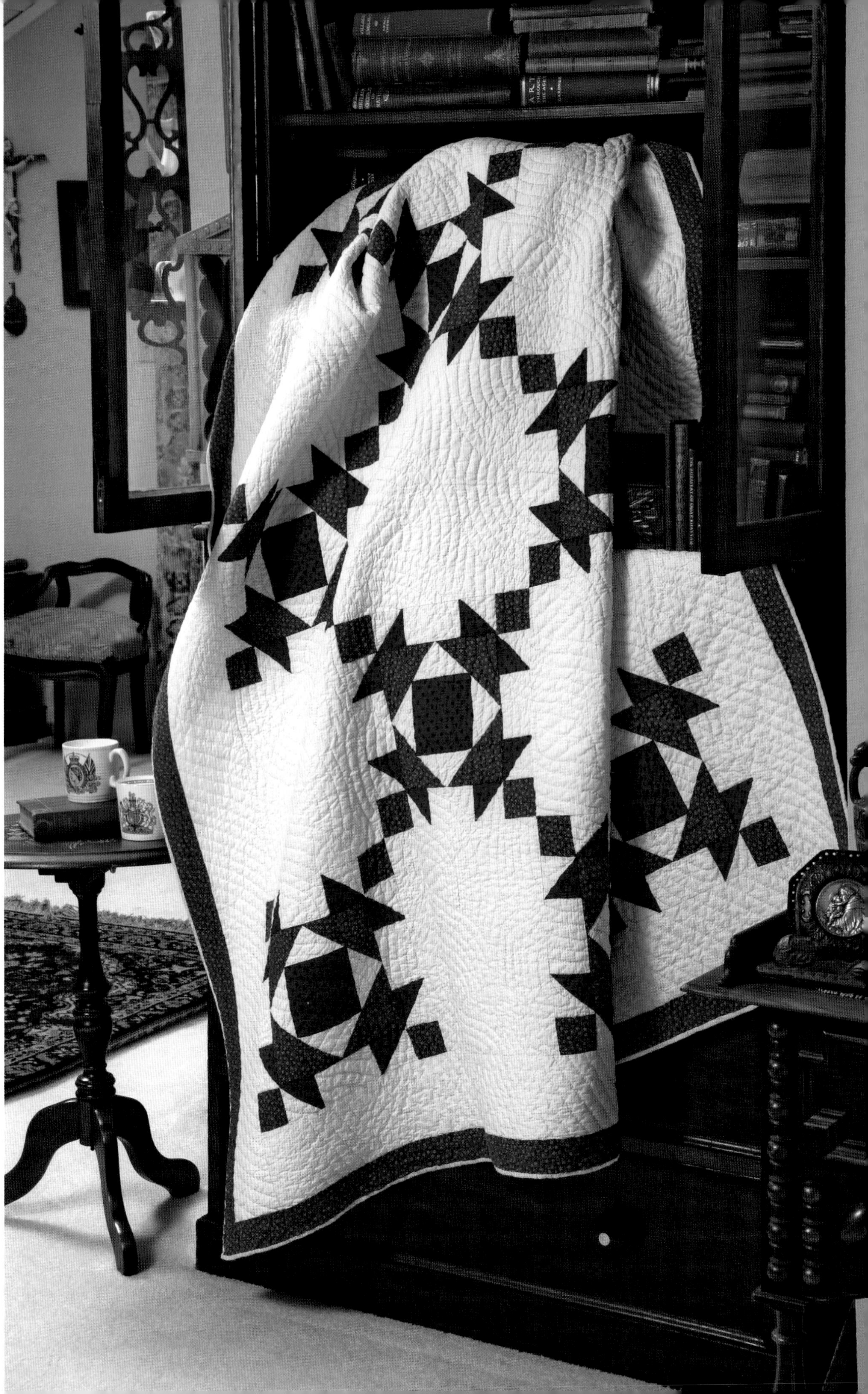

Mystery Quilt

The Mystery Quilt block is like someone you pass on a street — she looks familiar, but you just can't place her. This block looks like any number of blocks; it's just squares, triangles and rectangles (Figure 1). But it's just a bit different than other blocks; the triangles are turned another way, or there is a square instead of a triangle or a triangle instead of a square. The only place this block is actually shown is in *5,500 Quilt Block Designs* by Maggie Malone, where it's called Mystery Block and attributed to no particular source. Even the early quiltmaker had trouble with this mystery design. One block is smaller than all the others. She quickly solved her problem by adding strips to two sides to make it fit with the rest.

Even without a name, this quilt can be dated to the latter part of the 19th century because of the fabrics used in piecing. Here is the same green fabric used in Irish Chain on page 50 and of the same era as the one used in Flower Basket on page 42. And, the fabrics in this quilt are in the same "like-new" condition as both of these other quilts. The pencil marks used to trace the quilting designs are still visible across the top. There is only one real blemish on this quilt — an unusual one at that. This quilt was purchased from a well-known antique quilt dealer who washes her quilts before sale. What she didn't realize was that a leaf was trapped underneath when she placed the quilt outside to dry. As it dried, the tannins from the leaf leached into the backing of the quilt and left a perfect imprint of the leaf.

Figure 1

MAKE THE ANTIQUE QUILT

Finished Quilt Size 71½" Square
Finished Block Size 12" Square
Number of Blocks 13

MATERIALS

Based on 42"-wide fabric.

Red print ¾ yard

Green print 1⅜ yards

Muslin 4 yards

Backing 4½ yards

Batting 78" square

Coordinating thread

Rotary-cutting tools

CUTTING INSTRUCTIONS

Red print–fabric-width strips

- 2 strips 4½"; cut into thirteen 4½" A squares.
- 4 strips 2⅞"; cut into fifty-two 2⅞" D squares.

Green print–fabric-width strips

- 4 strips 4⅞"; cut into twenty-six 4⅞" squares. Cut squares on 1 diagonal to make 52 C triangles.
- 4 strips 2½"; cut into fifty-two 2½" G squares.
- 7 strips 2" for K and L borders

Muslin–fabric-width strips

- 3 strips 3⅜"; cut into twenty-six 3⅜" squares. Cut squares on 1 diagonal to make 52 B triangles.
- 4 strips 2⅞"; cut into fifty-two 2⅞" E squares.
- 4 strips 4½"; cut into fifty-two 2½" x 4½" F rectangles.
- 4 strips 12½"; cut into twelve 12½" H squares.
- 7 strips 4¾" for I and J borders
- 8 strips 2¼" or 2½" for binding

Use ¼" seam allowance for piecing. Arrows indicate pressing direction.

PIECING THE BLOCKS

1. Sew a B triangle to each side of A and press (Diagram 1). Repeat to make 13 A-B units.

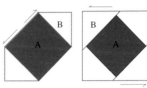

Diagram 1

2. Sew a C triangle to each side of each A-B unit and press (Diagram 2).

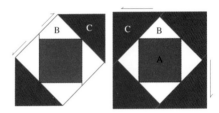

Diagram 2

3. Draw a diagonal line from corner to corner on the wrong side of each E square.

4. Place E right sides together with D; stitch ¼" from each side of the marked line, cut apart on the marked line and press to complete two D-E units (Diagram 3). Repeat to make 104 D-E units.

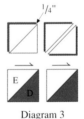

Diagram 3

5. Sew D-E to each end of each F strip and press (Diagram 4).

Diagram 4

6. Sew a D-E-F unit to opposite sides of an A-B-C unit and press to make a center row (Diagram 5). Repeat for 13 center rows.

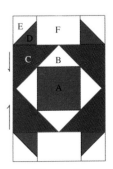

Diagram 5

7. Sew a G square to each end of the remaining D-E-F units and press to make 26 side rows (Diagram 6).

Diagram 6

8. Sew a side row to opposite long sides of a center row to complete one block referring to the Block Diagram; press seams toward the side rows. Repeat to make 13 blocks.

ASSEMBLING THE TOP

1. Join three blocks with two H squares to make a row; press seams toward H. Repeat for three rows.

2. Join two blocks with three H squares to make a row; press seams toward H. Repeat for two rows.

3. Join the rows referring to the Assembly Diagram for positioning of rows; press seams in one direction.

4. Join the I/J strips on short ends to make a long strip; press seams in one direction. Cut into two 60 1/2" I strips and two 69" J strips.

5. Sew an I strip to opposite sides and the J strips to the remaining sides; press seams toward strips.

6. Join the K/L strips on short ends to make a long strip; press seams in one direction. Cut into two 69" K strips and two 72" L strips.

7. Sew a K strip to opposite sides and the L strips to the remaining sides; press seams toward strips.

FINISHING

1. Piece backing to create a 78" square.

2. Mark top for quilting, sandwich quilt layers, hand- or machine-quilt and bind edges referring to the General Quiltmaking Instructions.

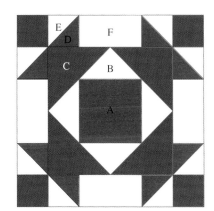
Block Diagram
12" Square
Make 13

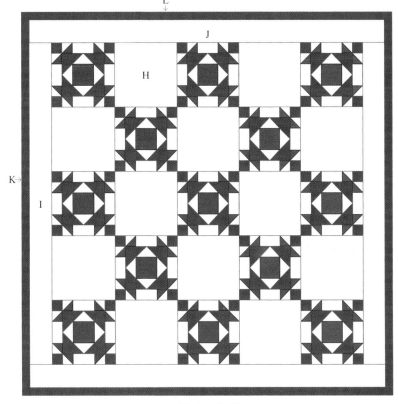
Mystery Quilt
Assembly Diagram 71 1/2" Square

Give It A Try...

Make a small sample to give this pattern a try. The blocks form a unique secondary pattern when joined without sashing. The simple pieced border repeats block elements to add a nice finishing touch.

- Purchase extra fabric to match your quilt or dig into your stash for a completely different look.

- Referring to quilt Cutting Instructions on page 70, cut 4 A squares, 16 E squares and eight 2½" border squares from red print. Cut 8 C squares, 16 G squares and two strips each 2½" x 28½" and 2½" x 32½" for borders from green print. Cut 8 B squares, 16 D squares, 16 F rectangles, four 2½" border squares and four 2½" x 24½" border strips from muslin. Cut squares into triangles as directed.

- Complete four blocks referring to the Block Diagram and Piecing the Blocks instructions on page 71. Join the blocks in two rows and join the rows to complete the center.

- Draw a diagonal line from corner to corner on the wrong side of each red border square.

- Place a square right sides together on each end of each muslin border strip, stitch on the marked line, trim seam allowance to ¼" and press the red triangle to the right side (Diagram 1).

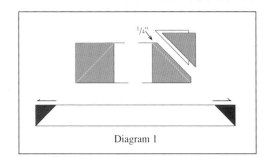

Diagram 1

- Sew a pieced strip to opposite sides of the center; press seams toward strips.

- Sew a muslin border square to each end of the two remaining pieced strips; press seams toward the squares.

- Sew the pieced strips to the remaining sides of the center.

- Sew the shorter green border strips to opposite sides and the longer strips to the remaining sides of the center to complete the sample.

1901–1940 Quilts

During the period from 1901 to 1940, the world changed. What began as an industrial surge in the early part of this period became a terrible depression that shook the very foundations of our country. People went from relative prosperity and good times to complete devastation and very hard times.

In the early part of the 20th century, quilters were using up leftovers from earlier years. The crazy quilts from the later 1800s and early 1900s were made more for show than for use and durability. Many of the pink and navy fabrics from the 19th century were still in use. It's easy to understand why quilting lost its popularity in the early 1900s when manufactured bedding became readily available. Buying bedding instead of making it gave busy women more time away from household chores.

World War 1 changed the focus of the country and refocused the energy of its women. Homemakers were encouraged to make quilts for use at home and to send blankets overseas with American soldiers. These practical quilts for use on the home front came to be known as "Liberty Quilts." Women also continued the tradition of making fund-raising autograph quilts to provide money to the boys overseas. These quilts worked to make money in two ways: people donated money to have their signatures on the quilt, and then the finished quilt was sold or raffled. The price for a signature might vary depending on where the signature was placed. The center space was usually the most expensive, twenty-five to fifty cents. Other spots were often ten cents. Red and white was the most popular combination for these quilts.

After World War 1, life for the homemaker became ever easier. Electric household appliances, such as washing machines, refrigerators and irons, were common in homes by the 1930s. With the extra time on their hands, women discovered their appreciation for handmade items again, including quilts. New quilt designs were published in the ever-

increasing world of magazines and books, and as time went by, published patterns became common-place in newspapers. A stitcher could purchase a whole kit including pattern, fabrics and batting to complete a quilt. Many companies sold patterns through mail order. The *Kansas City Star* began publishing quilt patterns in the late 1920s, and even the government sponsored programs to encourage arts and crafts including quilting through the Works Progress Administration, part of Franklin D. Roosevelt's "New Deal". The growth of state fairs saw an increase in quilt entries.

By 1920, quilting had become a national passion, and it grew. In 1933, 50,000 people attended a Mountain Mist quilt exhibit in Detroit, and that same year, Sears, Roebuck & Co., announced a quilt competition that eventually had 25,000 entries all hoping to win the $1,000 grand prize. Compare that to *Good Housekeeping's* 1977 quilt contest with a $2,000 prize and only 9,000 entries to gauge the popularity of quilting during this earlier period.

The Depression had a big influence on the type of quilts made during the hard times. Patterns such as the Double Wedding Ring (Figure 1), Grandmother's Flower Garden, Cathedral Window and Yo-Yo were popular because they could be made with very small scraps of fabrics with beautiful results.

Figure 1

Women stitched alone in rural settings but made social contacts at quilting bees where they got together with other women to quilt. With over 35 percent of the population living on farms in 1935, farm women of this period were almost as isolated as their pioneer ancestors.

Art Nouveau and Art Deco styles emerged in home furnishings, including quilts. Quilt designers became known for their own styles. Ann Orr's graph-like pieced designs (Figure 2) and Marie Webster's beautiful floral designs were popular. These women had a great influence on the quilts of that period that survive today.

Figure 2

Ann Orr was one of the most prolific designers in all areas of needlework during this period. In addition to publishing her own line of pattern and design leaflets she was the needlework editor of *Good Housekeeping Magazine* for over 20 years.

Marie Webster operated a highly successful mail order pattern business, The Practical Patchwork Company, from her home in Marion, Indiana. In 1915, she wrote *Quilts:Their Story and How to Make Them*, the first book ever written on quiltmaking. Her home in Indiana is now the permanent home of the Quilters Hall of Fame and was declared a National Historic Landmark by the National Park Service.

Perhaps the most recognizable fabrics of this era are the feed-sack (Figure 3) prints put to use in household items and quilts during the Depression years. Plain, coarsely woven cotton muslin bags were first produced in the mid-19th century and pieced by frugal quilters to make quilt backings and foundations for Log Cabin quilts. Flour, sugar, feed,

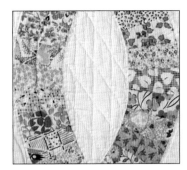
Figure 3

seeds, rice, fertilizer and tobacco were all sold in cloth bags. Larger sacks measured about 39" x 46" when split open while tobacco sacks were only 4" x 8". The quality of the cloth varied with the product; sugar sacks were more closely woven than rice sacks. Homemakers became adept at bleaching the sacks to remove the printed contents label and dyeing the fabric to use in household items and clothing. Solid-color sacks became available in the 1920s in several popular colors of the time: green, orange and yellow. Printed sacks were first introduced in the early 1930s. Patterns were printed to take advantage of feed-sack prints. Manufacturers began to compete to provide attractive bags to create customer loyalty. Sacks were printed in series, in popular themes and even preprinted for use as specific items like aprons and pillowcases. By 1949, Sears, Roebuck & Co., was advertising feed sacks in its catalog, and women across the United States were using these fabrics in hundreds of household items.

For those quilters who might want to recreate these quilts from the early part of the 20th century, a number of reproduction fabrics are now available, some of which appear in Figure 4.

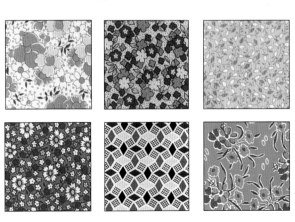
Figure 4

*B*roken Wheel

Turkey red-and-white quilts were very popular between 1880 and 1920. Many quilts in this combination were made during this period. Turkey red was very popular with quilters because it was colorfast and could be depended on not to run or bleed into the white fabric. It was widely available from such sources as Montgomery Ward and Sears, Roebuck & Co. Figure 1 shows the Broken Wheel block. However, these

Figure I

quilts did not stay in fashion after 1925. The red did not fit into the more pastel color palette that became popular from the late 1920s into the 1930s.

These red-and-white quilts also made perfect backgrounds for beautiful hand quilting. Though the piecing in this Broken Wheel quilt is far from perfect, the hand quilting is wonderful (Figure 2). Tiny stitches fill all the white areas of the quilt in many different quilting designs (Figure 3). Two of these designs, given with the quilt instructions, can be easily used as machine-quilting patterns.

Figure 2

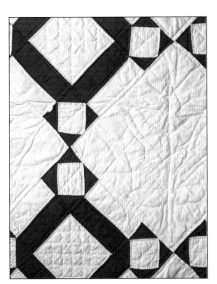

Figure 3

MAKE THE ANTIQUE QUILT

Finished Quilt Size 79" x 88¼"
Finished Block Size 11½" Square
Number of Blocks 20

MATERIALS

Based on 42"-wide fabric.

Red solid 2 yards

Muslin 6½ yards

Backing 5½ yards

Batting 85" x 95"

Coordinating thread

Rotary-cutting tools

CUTTING INSTRUCTIONS

Refer to Diagram 1 for cutting squares into triangles.

Diagram 1

Red solid–fabric-width strips

- 10 strips 2¼" for B

- 18 strips 2¼"; cut into three-hundred-twenty 2¼" E squares.

Muslin–fabric-width strips

- 3 strips 5"; cut into twenty 5" A squares.

- 10 strips 2¼" for C

- 8 strips 4"; cut into eighty 4" D squares.

- 4 strips 12"; cut into twelve 12" F squares.

- 2 strips 17½"; cut into four 17½" G squares and two 9" H squares. Cut G squares on both diagonals to make 14 G triangles and H squares on 1 diagonal to make 4 H triangles.

- 6 strips 7½" for I and J borders

- 9 strips 2¼" or 2½" for binding

Use ¼" seam allowance for piecing. Arrows indicate pressing direction.

PIECING THE BLOCKS

1. Draw a diagonal line from corner to corner on the wrong side of each E square.

2. Place an E square right sides together on one corner of D, stitch on the marked line, trim seam to ¼" and press E to the right side (Diagram 2). Repeat on remaining corners of D to complete a D-E unit. Repeat to make 80 D-E units.

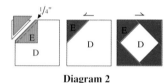

Diagram 2

3. Sew a B strip to a C strip to make a pieced strip (Diagram 3); press. Repeat to make 10 pieced strips.

4. Cut the pieced strips into eighty 5" B-C units (Diagram 3).

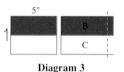

Diagram 3

5. Sew a B-C unit to opposite sides of A and press to complete a block center row (Diagram 4). Repeat to make 20 rows.

Diagram 4

6. Sew a D-E unit to opposite sides of a B-C unit and press to complete a block side row (Diagram 5). Repeat to make 40 rows.

Diagram 5

7. Sew a center row between two side rows to complete one block referring to the Block Diagram for positioning of rows; press seams toward the center row. Repeat to make 20 blocks.

ASSEMBLING THE TOP

Refer to the Assembly Diagram as needed for the following instructions.

1. Join blocks with F squares and G and H triangles in rows (Diagram 6); press seams away from blocks.

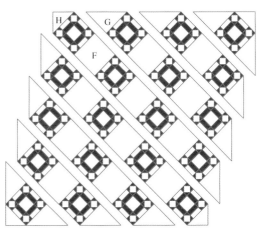

Diagram 6

2. Trim red seam allowances narrower behind the F squares to avoid red shadowing through the muslin (Diagram 7).

Diagram 7

3. Join the rows to complete the center referring to the Assembly Diagram on the next page for positioning of rows; press seams in one direction. Trim seam allowances.

4. Join the I/J strips on short ends to make a long strip; press seams in one direction. Cut into two 65½" I strips and two 88¾" J strips.

5. Sew the I strips to the top and bottom of the center and the J strips to opposite long sides; press seams toward strips.

FINISHING

1. Piece backing to create an 85" x 95" rectangle.

2. Mark top for quilting, sandwich quilt layers, hand- or machine-quilt and bind edges referring to the General Quiltmaking Instructions . Use the quilting designs given on pages 80 and 81 for F squares and G triangles and a cable design in the borders to duplicate the antique quilt.

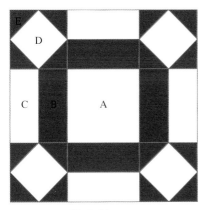

Block Diagram
11½" Square
Make 20

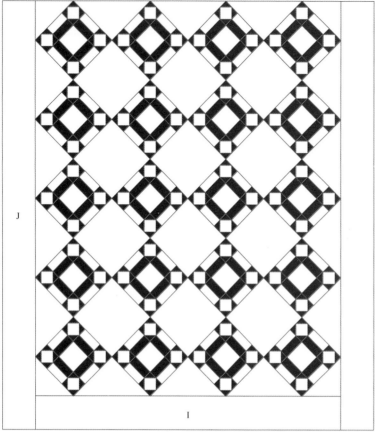

Broken Wheel
Assembly Diagram 79" x 88¹/₄"

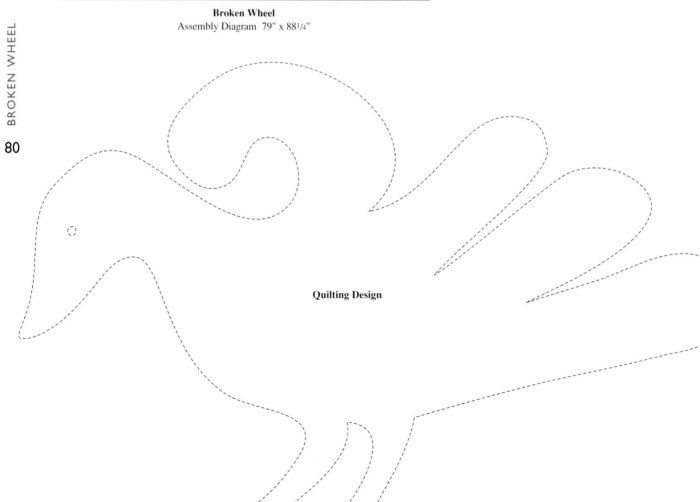

Quilting Design

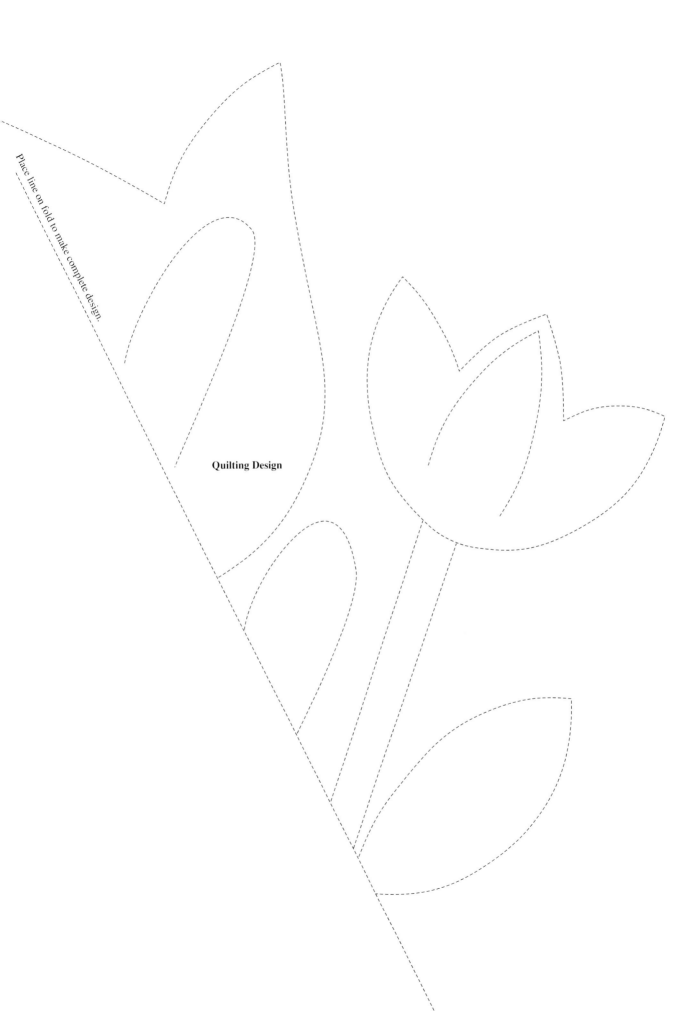

Quilting Design

Give It A Try...

With the variety of fabrics available today, a two-color quilt definitely doesn't have to be plain.

- Referring to quilt Cutting Instructions on page 78, cut 4 A squares, 16 D squares, 2 C strips, 16 E squares and four border strips 4" x 23½" from light fabric.

- Cut 2 B strips, 64 E squares, 4 D squares and two border strips each 4" x 30½" and 4" x 37½" from dark fabric.

- Complete four blocks referring to Piecing the Blocks on page 78.

- Join the blocks in two rows and join the rows to complete the center; press seams in one direction.

- Complete four D-E units using dark D squares and light E squares.

- Sew a light border strip to opposite sides of the center; press seams toward strips.

- Sew a D-E unit to each end of the remaining light border strips; press seams toward strips. Sew a strip to the remaining sides of the center; press seams toward strips.

- Sew the dark border strips to opposite sides and then to the remaining sides; press seams toward strips to complete the sample.

Double Wedding Ring

The Double Wedding Ring pattern has been traced to as long ago as 1825 — a quilt of this pattern and age is part of the collection of the Shelburne Museum in Vermont. It was published in an 1895 catalog of the Ladies Art Co., as a single-block design. However, this pattern is most often attributed to quilts made during the Depression. It was during this time that the pattern took on the look that is so common today: wedges pieced into an arc shape and joined with plain squares to form Four Patches between the arcs as they are arranged into the interlocking-ring shapes (Figure 1).

Figure 1

Quilters of those frugal years pounced on the opportunity to use the available feed sack fabric in all those small arc pieces with just a small addition of the popular pastel solids in the Four Patches. The ring shapes were then either appliquéd on a large white background or pieced into a whole top with white fabric shapes between the arc pieces and in the center of the rings. Often the edges of the quilt followed the shape of the rings. The quilt shown here used a combination of these methods. The rings were pieced to form the center and then appliquéd onto a white border frame. The plain white spaces gave the quiltmaker a spot to practice her quilting ability (Figure 2). The quiltmaker added a unique touch to the straight edges of this quilt by adding two layers of prairie points, one of the prints used in the arcs and the other white (Figure 3).

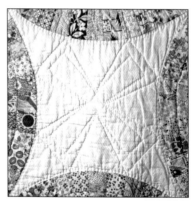

Figure 2

Figure 3

MAKE THE ANTIQUE QUILT
Finished Quilt Size 70" x 84¼"

MATERIALS
Based on 42"-wide fabric.

Green solid ¼ yard

Coral solid ¼ yard

Assorted prints (at least 11) 4½ yards total

White solid 7½ yards

Backing 5¼ yards

Batting 76" x 90"

Coordinating thread

Template materials

Rotary-cutting tools

CUTTING INSTRUCTIONS

Green solid–fabric-width strips
- 2 strips 2¾"; cut into twenty-four 2¾" D squares.

Coral solid–fabric-width strips
- 2 strips 2¾"; cut into twenty-four 2¾" E squares.

Assorted prints
- Cut one-hundred-twenty-two 3" H squares. If using yardage, cut nine 3" fabric-width strips and cut into one-hundred-twenty-two 3" H squares.
- Cut remaining fabric into 3"-wide by any length strips. If using yardage, cut forty 3" fabric-width strips total.

White solid–fabric-width strips
- 4 strips 2¾"; cut into fifty-six 2¾" C squares.
- 9 strips 3"; cut into one-hundred-twenty-two 3" I squares.

White solid–fabric-length strips
- 2 strips 8½" x 85⅛" F borders along length of fabric
- 2 strips 8½" x 70⅞" G borders along length of fabric

White solid
- Make templates and cut A and B pieces as directed on patterns given, cutting alignment notches into seam allowances.

Use ¼" seam allowance for piecing. Arrows indicate pressing direction.

PIECING THE ARCS

1. Trace the proper number of Arc patterns and cut out, leaving a margin of paper around the edges.

2. Beginning at the end of one Arc pattern, place a print strip on the unmarked side to cover segment 1, extending ¼" into the second segment and covering the end seam allowance (Diagram 1).

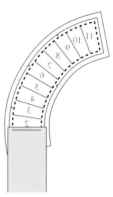

Diagram 1

3. Place a second strip right sides together with the first (Diagram 2); pin in place.

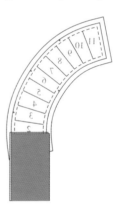

Diagram 2

4. Flip the pattern over and stitch on the marked line between the segments, extending stitching to the outer solid line on each end (Diagram 3).

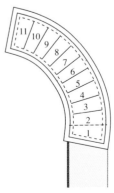

Diagram 3

5. Trim the seam allowance to ¼" if necessary (Diagram 4); fold the top strip over to cover segment 2 and press.

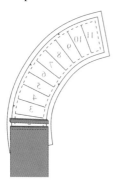

Diagram 4

6. Trim the long end of the segment 1 strip, leaving enough to cover the end seam allowance and trim the segment 2 strip, leaving ¼" extending into segment 3 (Diagram 5).

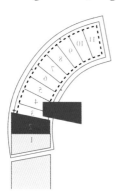

Diagram 5

7. Place another strip right sides together with strip 2, pin, flip pattern over and stitch on the marked line between segments 2 and 3. Trim seam allowance, fold the top strip to cover segment 3, press and trim strip end.

8. Continue with additional strips to cover the remaining segments to complete one Arc (Diagram 6); repeat to make 98 Arcs.

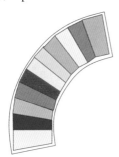

Diagram 6

9 Trim paper and fabric on the outside solid line of the patterns, cutting alignment notches into seam allowances. Remove paper.

PIECING THE UNITS

1. Center and sew an Arc to B, matching notches and clipping curves (Diagram 7); press. Repeat with all B pieces.

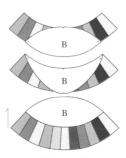

Diagram 7

2. Sew a C square to each end of 25 Arcs and press (Diagram 8). Repeat with D and E squares on opposite ends of the remaining Arcs (Diagram 8); press.

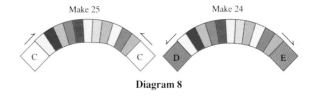

Diagram 8

3. Center and sew a C-Arc to the remaining side of a B piece to make a C unit (Diagram 9); press. Repeat to make 25 C units.

4. Repeat step 3 with D-E-Arcs on the remaining B pieces to make 24 D-E units (Diagram 9); press.

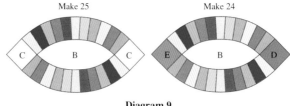

Diagram 9

ASSEMBLING THE TOP

Refer to the Assembly Diagram as needed for the following instructions.

1. Center and sew a C unit to one side of each A piece, matching notches and clipping curves (Diagram 10); press.

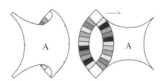

Diagram 10

2. Join 4 A-C units with one C unit to make a row (Diagram 11); press. Repeat to make 5 A-C rows.

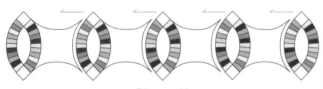

Diagram 11

3. Arrange four D-E units in a row (Diagram 12); repeat for six D-E rows.

Diagram 12

4. Sew the D-E rows into the A-C rows, beginning and ending with a D-E row and referring to the Assembly Diagram for positioning of rows; press seams toward the A-C rows.

5. Turn under the edge of the pieced center 1/4" all around; baste in place.

6. Trim each end of the F and G border strips at a 45-degree angle (Diagram 13).

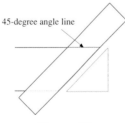

45-degree angle line

Diagram 13

7. Join the strips with mitered corners to make a frame (Diagram 14); press mitered seam open.

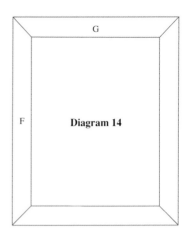

G

F

Diagram 14

8. Place the frame right side up on a flat surface and smooth. Place the pieced center right side up on the frame with the edges of the Arcs 3" from the outside edge of the frame and the seam between the C and D squares aligned with the mitered corner seams (Diagram 15); when even, pin in place all around.

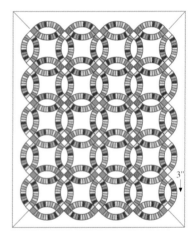

3"

Diagram 15

9. Hand- or machine-stitch the edges of the pieced center to the frame all around; press. Trim away excess frame under pieced center to leave a 1/4" seam allowance. Remove basting.

FINISHING

1. Piece backing to create a 76" x 90" rectangle.

2. Mark top for quilting, sandwich quilt layers and hand- or machine-quilt referring to the General Quiltmaking Instructions, leaving 1" unquilted around edge of top. Use the quilting design given in the center of each A to duplicate the antique quilt as seen in Figure 2 on page 85.

3. Trim batting 1/4" narrower than top all around; trim backing 1/4" wider than top. Fold backing

and batting back away from edge all around; pin to hold to prevent backing and batting from being stitched with prairie points.

4. Press each H and I square in half diagonally twice to make prairie points (Diagram 16).

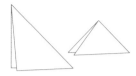

Diagram 16

5. Place 33 H pieces on one long side with raw edges aligned, beginning with the tip of H aligned with one end of the side and with H tips touching along the length (Diagram17); pin in place. The last H tip will not reach the end of the side.

Diagram 17

6. Starting at the opposite end of the same side, place 33 I pieces along the length of the border as for the H pieces (Diagram 18); pin in place. The points of the I pieces should be centered between the points of the H pieces.

Diagram 18

7. Baste pieces in place 1/8" from edge.

8. Repeat steps 5-7 on the opposite long side. Repeat on each end with 28 each H and I pieces, overlapping triangle tips as needed to center the I pieces between the H pieces.

9. Stitch all around edge of top using a 1/4" seam allowance.

10. Trim prairie point seam allowance at the corners of the top to 1/8" to reduce bulk.

11. Fold prairie points to outside edge of top and seam allowance to back and press. Machine-baste 1/8" inside edge of top all around to hold seam allowance in place.

12. Unpin backing and batting; turn backing edge in 1/2" all around, enclosing edge of batting. Hand-stitch in place to wrong side of top.

13. Hand- or machine-quilt a line of stitches 1/8"-1/4" inside edge of top and as desired in remaining unquilted area. Remove basting.

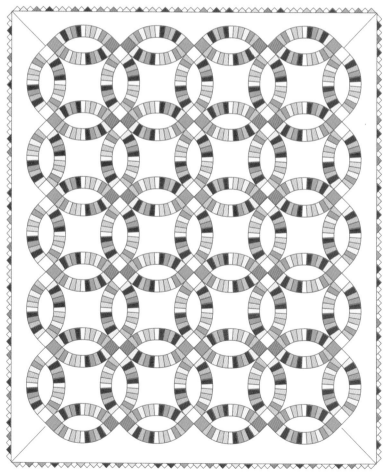

Double Wedding Ring
Assembly Diagram 70" x 84¼"

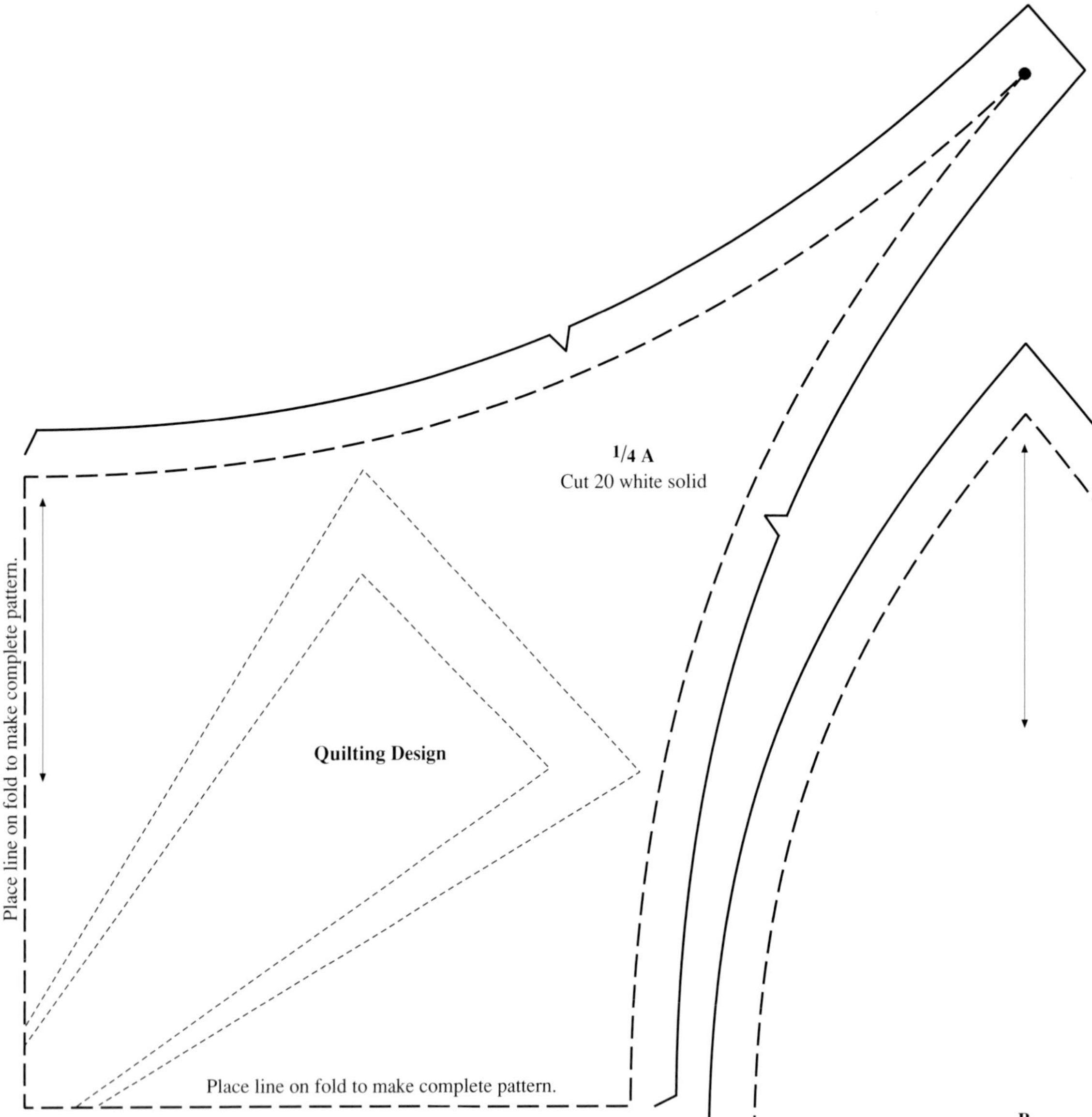

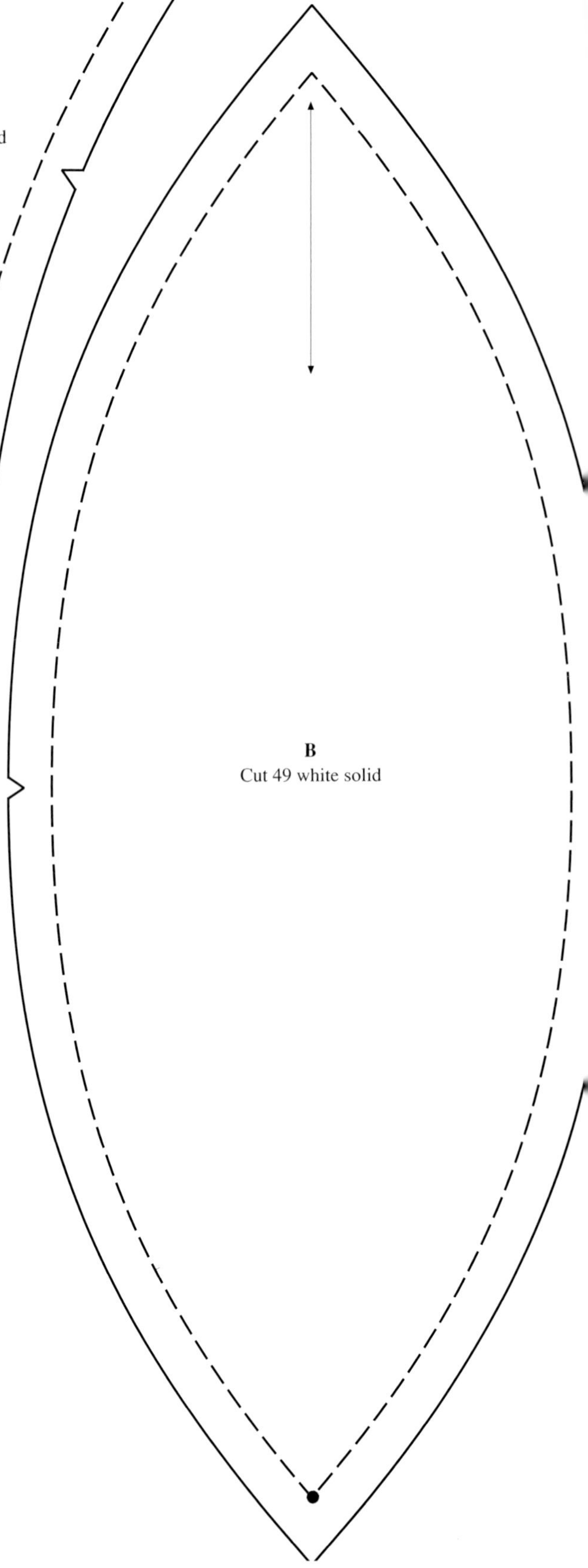

1/4 A
Cut 20 white solid

Place line on fold to make complete pattern.

Quilting Design

Place line on fold to make complete pattern.

B
Cut 49 white solid

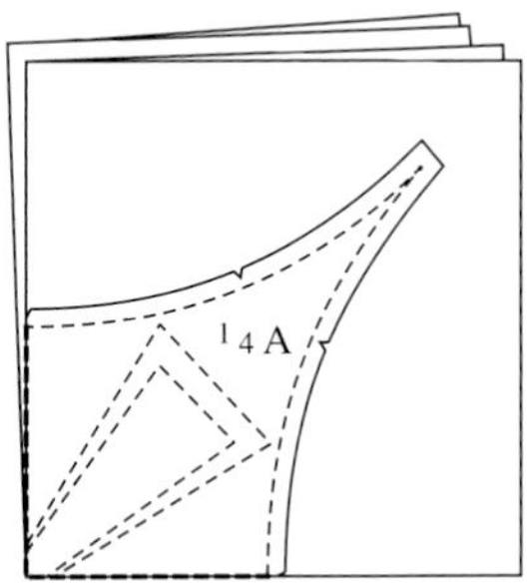

^{1}4 A

To make complete A pattern, fold a 14" square
of paper in half twice. Make a paper template of
the ^{1}4 A pattern; place on the folded paper with
the dashed edges of the ^{1}4 A pattern aligned
with the folds of the paper. Trace the solid-line
edges of the pattern onto the paper. Cut out on
traced lines to make A pattern.

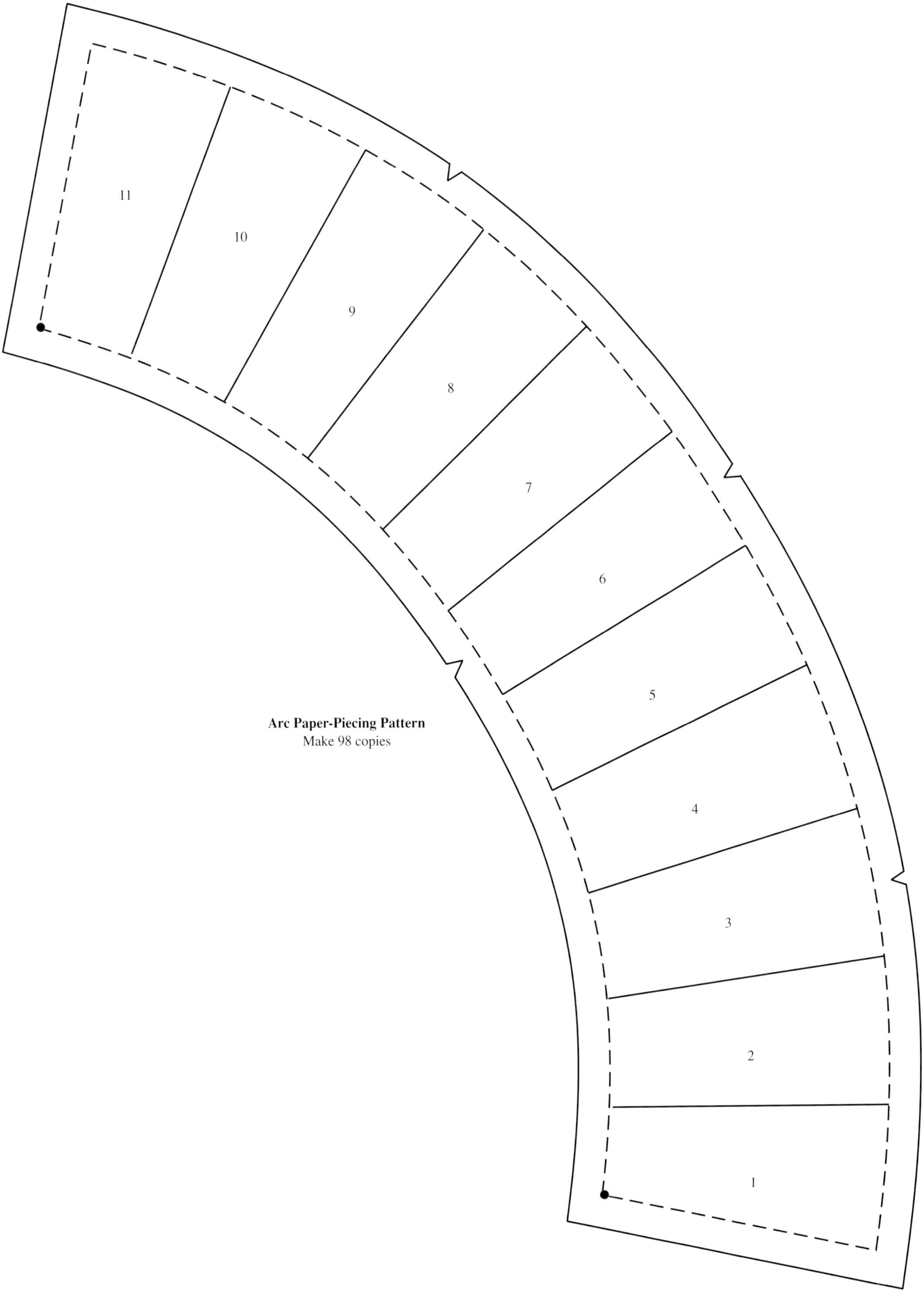

Arc Paper-Piecing Pattern
Make 98 copies

11

10

9

8

7

6

5

4

3

2

1

Give It A Try...

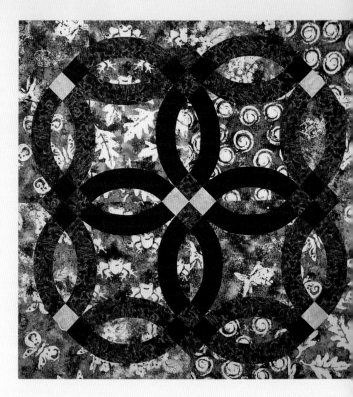

Love the look of the Double Wedding Ring but hate the curved piecing? Use fusible web to attach the Arc and C, D and E squares to a background. Use the Arc Paper-Piecing Pattern to cut one fabric Arc shape. You will need 4¾ yards of 12"-wide double-stick fusible web for this sample. The antique quilt uses three different solids for the squares at the ends of the Arcs: white for C squares, green for D squares and coral for E squares. The sample project also uses three fabrics for these pieces: cream for C, green for D and magenta for E. It also uses the D and E fabrics for the Arc shapes. The C, D and E labels in the following instructions refer to the fabric used, not the piece. For example, a D square or D Arc is one cut from the D fabric (green). If you choose fabrics in different colors for your sample, be sure to label each fabric with C, D or E to aid in cutting and placing the pieces.

- Cut or piece a 42" background square. The sample was pieced with an assortment of 11" squares set in four rows of four squares each.

- Fold the background in quarters and press to mark the vertical and horizontal centerlines. Refold diagonally twice and press to mark the diagonal centerlines.

- Prepare a template for the Arc shape using the inner dashed line for the outside edge of the template.

- Trace 24 Arcs on the paper side of the fusible web that will be removed last (see manufacturer's instructions); cut out leaving a margin around each one. Remove paper liner.

- Place 16 Arcs on the wrong side of the E fabric and eight on the D fabric; lightly press just to hold; cut out shapes on marked lines.

- Cut seven 2½" x 12" strips fusible web; remove liner and lightly fuse two strips to the wrong side of the C and D fabrics and three to the E fabric.

- Trim one edge of the fused fabric to even the fusible web and fabric edges; cut into six 2¼" C squares, 10 D squares and 12 E squares. Remove paper from pieces.

- Place two C and D squares on-point in the center of the background so the points touch but do not overlap (Diagram 1); finger-press in place.

- Measure 8" along the vertical and horizontal centerlines and make a small mark on the centerline; place two fabric-E Arcs along each line with one end of each Arc evenly aligned with the center C or D square and the inside corner of the opposite end at the 8" mark (Diagram 2). Finger-press in place.

- Place two D and E squares on-point into the intersection of these Arc pairs with the points of the D squares aligned with the creased centerlines and the E squares evenly aligned with the edges of the D squares; finger-press in place.

- Measure 8" in a straight line from the outside corner of each of these E squares toward a diagonal centerline and make a mark; place two D-fabric Arcs from the corner of the E square to the 8" mark (Diagram 3). Finger-press in place. Repeat at each 8" mark.

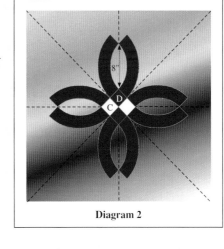

Diagram 1

- Place a C or E square into the intersection of each set of these Arc pieces with the outside edge of each square aligned with the diagonal centerline (Diagram 4); finger-press in place.

- Adjust any piece as necessary to evenly align all edges. When satisfied with positioning, fuse all pieces in place (see manufacturer's instructions).

- Machine-stitch the edges of each piece in place using thread and stitch of choice. The sample was stitched with a narrow zigzag stitch and invisible thread.

- Trim edges of background square 2" from the outer edge of the arcs. The background should measure 40" square. Add borders as desired to complete the sample top.

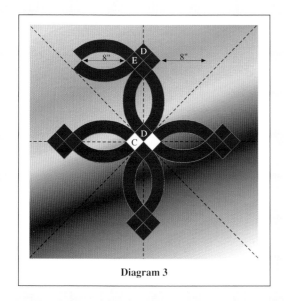

Diagram 3

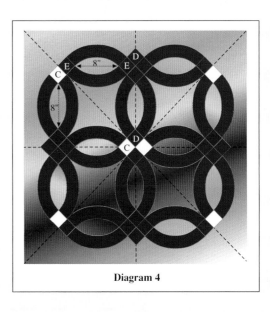

Diagram 2

Diagram 4

Framed Nine-Patch

The pink and green solids used with the scrappy Nine-Patch blocks in this Framed Nine-Patch quilt are typical of the colors used in the 1930s era (Figure 1). The green is not the prettiest color, and is rarely found today, but during this period of our quiltmaking heritage, it was a most popular choice. It was also a popular color for painted furniture and inside woodwork of homes of this time period. Figure 2 shows a section of the framing with the quilting design.

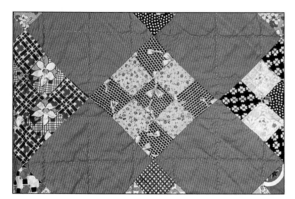

Figure 1

Figure 2

MAKE THE ANTIQUE QUILT

Finished Quilt Size 78" Square
Finished Block Size 3¾" Square
Number of Blocks 109

MATERIALS

Based on 42" fabric width. Nine-Patch blocks are made with scraps.

Assorted scraps or forty-four 1¾" x 18" strips light and fifty-five 1¾" x 18" strips dark for Nine-Patch blocks

Pink solid 2 yards

Green solid 3½ yards

Backing 4¾ yards

Batting 84" square

Coordinating thread

Rotary-cutting tools

CUTTING INSTRUCTIONS

Refer to Diagram 1 for cutting squares into triangles.

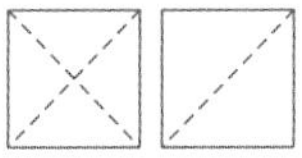

Diagram 1

Assorted Scraps

- Cut 436 light A and 545 dark B 1¾" squares

Pink solid–fabric-width strips

- 6 strips 4¼"; cut into forty-eight 4¼" C squares.

- 1 strip 6⅝"; cut into six 6⅝" squares. Cut each square on both diagonals to make 24 D triangles.

- 8 strips 3½"; cut into ninety-six 3½" squares. Cut each square on 1 diagonal to make 192 E triangles.

Green solid–fabric-width strips

- 4 strips 5¾" x 38" for F

- 6 strips 5½" for G

- 8 strips 5" for H

- 8 strips 2¼" or 2½" for binding

Use ¼" seam allowance for piecing. Arrows indicate pressing direction.

PIECING THE BLOCKS WITH SCRAPS

The same B fabric and the same A fabric are used in one block.

1. If using scrap squares to complete blocks, complete one block by joining one A and two B squares to make a row (Diagram 2); press. Repeat for two B-A-B rows.

2. Join one B and two A squares to make an A-B-A row (Diagram 2); press.

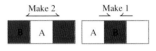

Diagram 2

3. Join the rows to complete one block (Diagram 3); press. Repeat for 109 blocks.

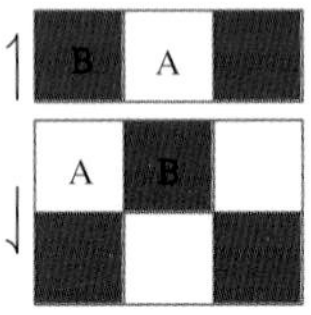

Diagram 3

PIECING BLOCKS WITH STRIPS

The same B fabric and the same A fabric are used in one block.

1. Sew an A strip between two B strips (Diagram 4); press. Cut pieced strip into ten 1¾" B-A-B segments (Diagram 4). Repeat for 22 B-A-B pieced strips; cut into 218 segments.

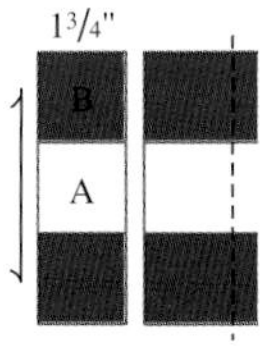

Diagram 4

2. Sew a B strip between two A strips (Diagram 5); press. Cut pieced strip into ten 1¾" A-B-A segments (Diagram 5). Repeat for 11 A-B-A pieced strips; cut into 109 segments.

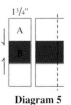

Diagram 5

3. Sew an A-B-A segment between two B-A-B segments to complete one block (Diagram 3); press. Repeat for 109 blocks.

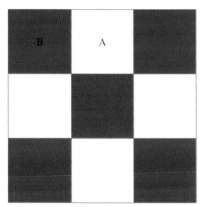

Block Diagram
3³/₄" Square
Make 109

COMPLETING BORDER BLOCKS

1. Sew an E triangle to each side of a Nine-Patch block (Diagram 6) to complete a border block; press. Repeat for 48 border blocks.

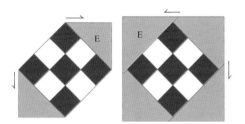

Diagram 6

ASSEMBLING THE TOP

Refer to the Assembly Diagram as needed for the following instructions.

1. Join four Nine-Patch blocks with three C squares to make a row; press seams toward C. Repeat for four rows.

2. Join three Nine-Patch blocks with four C squares to make a row; press seams toward C. Repeat for three rows.

3. Join the rows referring to the Assembly Diagram to complete the quilt center; press seams in one direction.

4. Center and sew an F strip to each side of the pieced center, mitering corners (Diagram 7); press. Trim excess mitered seam at corners to ¹/₄" (Diagram 8); press seams open.

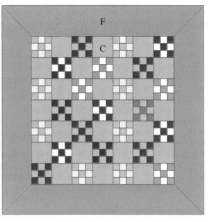

Diagram 7

Diagram 8

5. Join three Nine-Patch blocks with two C squares and one D triangle to make a row (Diagram 9); press. Repeat with blocks and C and D pieces to make remaining rows, again referring to Diagram 9; press.

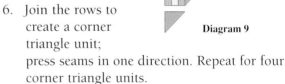

Diagram 9

6. Join the rows to create a corner triangle unit; press seams in one direction. Repeat for four corner triangle units.

7. Center and sew a corner triangle unit to each side of the quilt center (Diagram 10); press. Trim excess F strips even with corner units (Diagram 11).

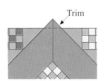

Diagram 11

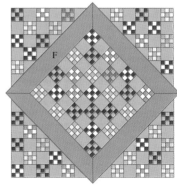

Diagram 10

FRAMED NINE-PATCH

97

8. Join G strips on short ends; press seams to one side. Cut into four 60" G strips. Center and sew a G strip to each side of the quilt center, mitering corners as in step 4; trim and press.

9. Join 11 border blocks to make a side border strip; press seams in one direction. Repeat for two strips. Sew a strip to opposite sides of the quilt center; press seams toward G strips.

10. Join 13 border blocks to make a top border strip; press seams in one direction. Repeat for bottom border strip. Sew a strip to the top and bottom of the quilt center; press seams toward G strips.

12. Join H strips on short ends; press seams to one side. Cut into four 80" H strips. Center and sew an H strip to each side of the quilt center, mitering corners as in step 4; trim and press.

FINISHING

1. Piece backing to create a 84" square.

2. Mark top for quilting, sandwich quilt layers, hand- or machine-quilt and bind edges referring to the General Quiltmaking Instructions. The quilt shown was hand-quilted in a 1¾" grid through the Nine-Patch areas and using the pattern given below in the borders.

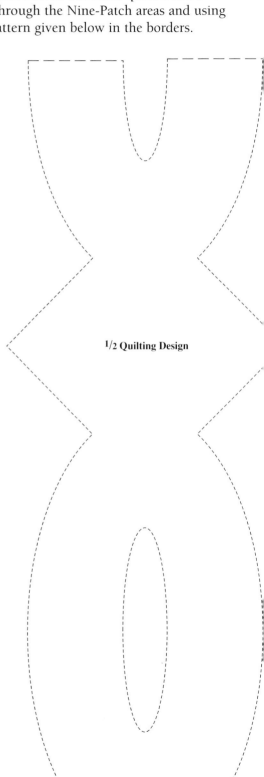

¹/₂ Quilting Design

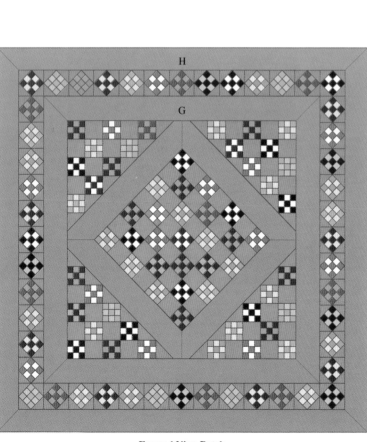

Framed Nine-Patch
Assembly Diagram 78" Square

Give It A Try...

If you prefer a more planned look for your Framed Nine-Patch quilt, purchase just two fabrics to create the blocks. To recreate the layout of the antique quilt, you would need approximately 1¼ yards light fabric and 1½ yards dark fabric to piece the Nine-Patch blocks, cutting twenty 1¾" fabric-width strips light fabric and twenty-five 1¾" fabric-width strips dark fabric. Refer to Piecing Blocks with Strips on page 96 for piecing instructions, except cut pieced strips into 24 segments.

The Give It A Try sample is pieced with 6" Nine-Patch blocks to make a larger center area and bordered with 2" and 4" strips with Nine-Patch blocks in the corners. As is, this piece could be used as a table cover or a wall hanging. Another option is to add more Nine-Patch blocks around this center with more borders to make a bed-size quilt. The color placement in these blocks is opposite the antique version with more light-color squares than dark in each block with dark setting squares. This type of quilt can be cut and pieced in a weekend.

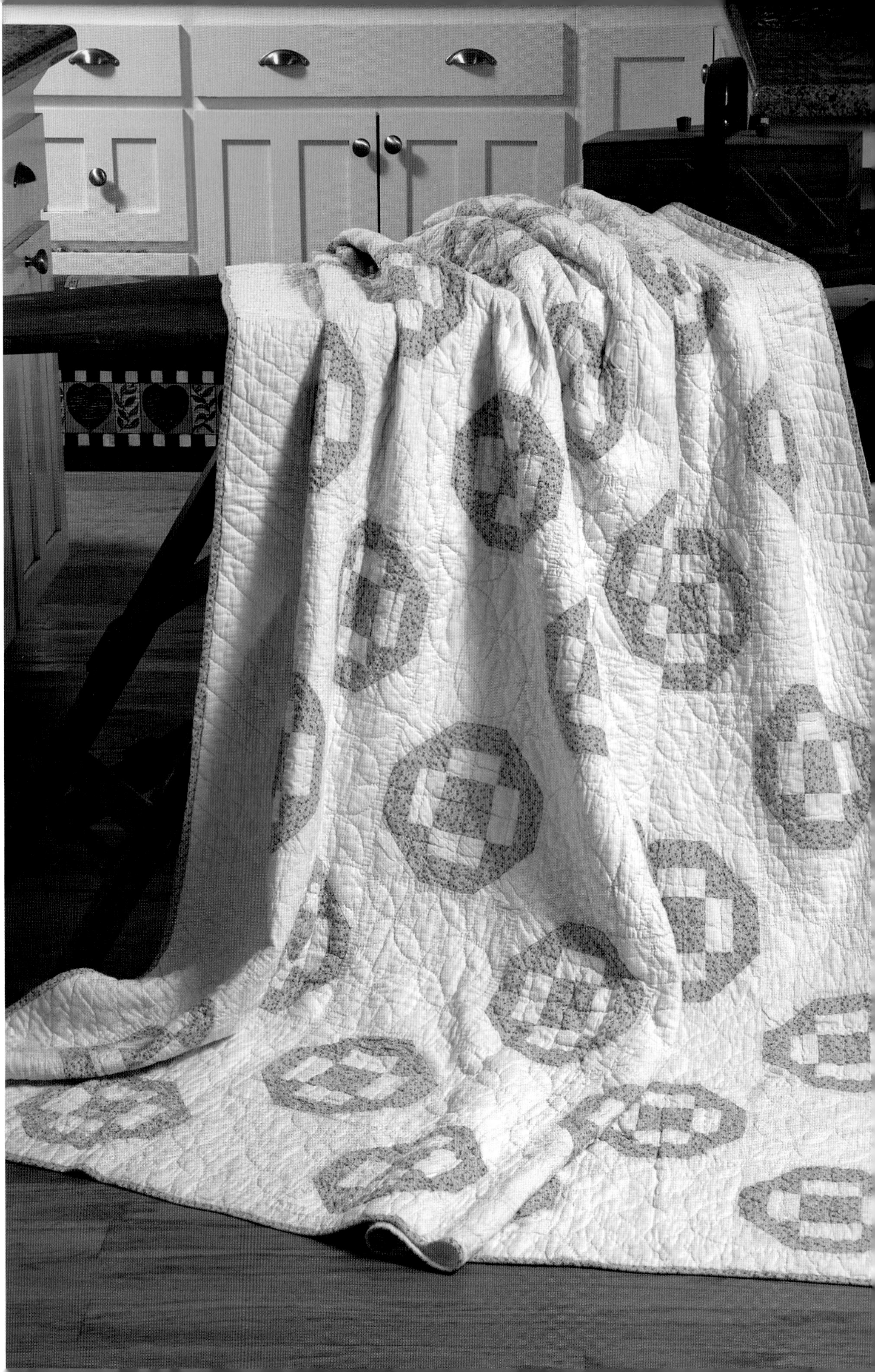

Grecian Square

The earliest mention of the Grecian Square design was by the Ladies Art Co. in 1897. Founded in the 1890s, the Ladies Art Co. is considered to be the first mail-order quilt pattern company to sell standardized patchwork patterns nationwide. The yellow calico print in this quilt was popular from the 1830s until the 1930s so it is very appropriate that a pattern published in 1897 be made with this fabric sometime around the turn of the century. Figure 1 shows the block.

The maker of this quilt seems to have had a problem deciding on the width of the borders. She began with a 4" border on one long side with a border 1½" at its narrowest to 3" at its widest on the other long side. Then she added a one-half inch 1½"-wide border on one end and a mostly 2" border on the other end. She also used an unusual binding technique: the binding was stitched to the top edge of the backing and turned to the front, leaving no binding visible on the back at all.

The large white areas of the quilt afforded the quilter the opportunity to do some fine quilting as shown in Figure 2. See page 104 for the pattern for this quilting design.

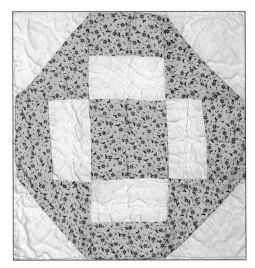

Figure 1

Figure 2

MAKE THE ANTIQUE QUILT

Finished Quilt Size 68" x 83"
Finished Block Size 7½" Square
Number of Blocks 40

MATERIALS

Based on 42"-wide fabric.

Yellow print 2¼ yards

Muslin 4½ yards

Backing 5¼ yards

Batting 74" x 89"

Coordinating thread

Rotary-cutting tools

CUTTING INSTRUCTIONS

Yellow print-fabric-width strips

- 3 strips 3"; cut into forty 3" A squares.
- 12 strips 1¾" for C
- 7 strips 3⅜"; cut into eighty 3⅜" E squares.
- 8 strips 2¼" or 2½" for binding

Muslin-fabric-width strips

- 12 strips 1¾" for B
- 7 strips 3⅜"; cut into eighty 3⅜" D squares.
- 8 strips 8"; cut into forty 8" F squares.
- 8 strips 4½" for G and H borders

Use ¼" seam allowance for piecing. Arrows indicate pressing direction.

PIECING THE BLOCKS

1. Draw a diagonal line from corner to corner on the wrong side of each D square.

2. Place a D square right sides together with an E square, stitch 1/4" from each side of the drawn line, cut apart on the line and press to complete two D-E units (Diagram 1). Repeat to complete 160 D-E units.

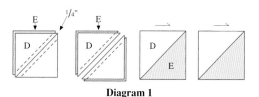

Diagram 1

3. Sew a B strip to a C strip to make a pieced strip (Diagram 2); press. Repeat to make 12 pieced strips.

4. Cut the pieced strips into one-hundred-sixty 3" B-C units (Diagram 2).

Diagram 2

5. Sew a B-C unit to opposite sides of A and press to complete a block center row (Diagram 3). Repeat to make 40 rows.

Diagram 3

6. Sew a D-E unit to opposite sides of a B-C unit and press to complete a block side row (Diagram 4). Repeat to make 80 rows.

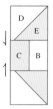

Diagram 4

7. Sew a center row between two side rows to complete one block referring to the Block Diagram for positioning of rows; press seams toward the center row. Repeat to make 40 blocks.

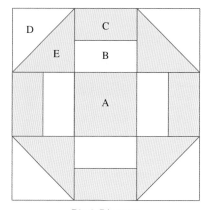

Block Diagram
7½" Square

ASSEMBLING THE TOP

Refer to the Assembly Diagram as needed for the following instructions.

1. Join four blocks with four F squares to make a row (Diagram 5); press. Repeat to make 10 rows.

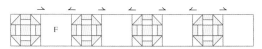

Diagram 5

2. Join the rows to complete the center referring to the Assembly Diagram for positioning of rows; press seams in one direction.

3. Join the G/H strips on short ends to make a long strip; press seams in one direction. Cut into two 75½" G strips and two 68½" H strips.

4. Sew the G strips to opposite long sides of the center and the H strips to the top and bottom; press seams toward strips.

FINISHING

1. Piece backing to create a 74" x 89" rectangle.

2. Mark top for quilting, sandwich quilt layers, hand- or machine-quilt and bind edges referring to the General Quiltmaking Instructions. Use four of the quilting design given in each F square to duplicate the antique quilt (Diagram 6).

Diagram 6

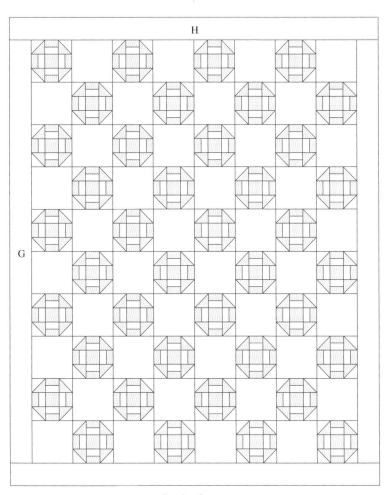

Grecian Square
Assembly Diagram 68" x 83"

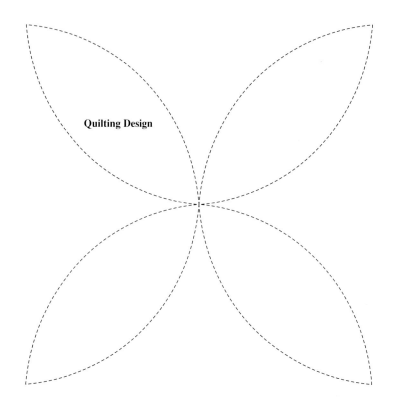

Quilting Design

Give It A Try...

Use three same-value fabrics instead of yellow in a block-to-block setting to create a very different look with the Grecian Square block. Use the strip-pieced B-C units to add a fitting border to this nine-block arrangement.

- Referring to quilt Cutting Instructions on page 102, cut 9 A squares and two border strips each 3" x 23" and 3" x 38" from one fabric.

- Cut 4 C strips and 10 E squares from a second fabric.

- Cut 3 C strips and 8 E squares from the third fabric.

- Cut 7 B strips, 18 D squares, four 3" squares for border corners and two border strips each 1¾" x 23", 1¾" x 25½", 1¾" x 30½" and 1¾" x 33" from background fabric.

- Complete four blocks of one fabric and five blocks of a second fabric referring to Piecing the Blocks on page 102. Cut 15 additional B-C units of each color combination.

- Join the blocks in three rows and join the rows to complete the center referring to the sample photo for positioning; press seams in one direction.

- Sew the 23" border strips to opposite sides and the 25½" strips to the remaining sides of the center; press seams toward strips.

- Join six B-C units of one color with four B-C units of the second color to make a strip (Diagram 1); press seams away from background. Repeat to make four strips.

- Sew a strip to opposite sides of the center; press seams toward background strips.

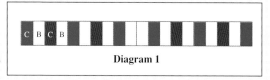

Diagram 1

- Sew the remaining 1¾" border strips to the sides and then the top and bottom of the center; press seams toward strips.

- Sew a border corner square to each end of the remaining pieced strips; press seams toward border squares. Sew a strip to the remaining sides of the center; press seams toward background strips.

- Sew the 3" border strips to the sides and then the top and bottom of the center to complete the sample; press seams toward strips.

Hexagon Bouquets

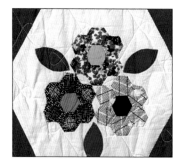

The wonderful thing about most old quilts is that the makers did not always worry about making something perfect. In this quilt, the quiltmaker simply cut whole blocks in half for the half blocks at the end. This means that the hexagon was 1/2" smaller because of the seam allowance lost at the center cutting line. To make the borders fit more perfectly, our instructions require half blocks that are cut and appliquéd as half blocks, and we had to change things slightly to make the border triangles meet at the corners to create a pleasing design. Mathematically, they should not work on the actual quilt, but they do. The quilter probably pulled and pinched here and there to make them work.

English paper-piecing is the preferred method to use when joining small hexagons to make flower shapes. This method involves cutting a paper shape the size of the finished hexagon and then wrapping the seam allowance edges of the fabric hexagon around it and pressing to hold in place. Freezer-paper, card-stock or heat-resistant Mylar shapes may be used. The pieces are joined with tiny, invisible stitches from the right side. You have to be careful not to catch the paper pieces in the stitching. Once the pieces are stitched into units, the freezer paper, card stock or heat-resistant Mylar is removed. This type of stitching is the kind of thing lots of quilters like to have as a long-term project that is always there to fill little snippets of time such as when waiting for an appointment. The pieces are small, so they are quite portable. This is not the type of project that a quilter tries to finish in a week.

Figure 1

The longer you look at the antique quilt, the more you notice that many of the flowers include a design centered in each hexagon petal to create an interesting flower. (See the close-ups in Figure 1.) These pieces were fussy cut on an identical area of a print scrap and pieced using paper foundations, or the English paper-piecing method. It is fun to discover the interesting motifs the quilter chose to make her flowers. Some have no centered elements and still others have stripes that run horizontal to the center while others are perpendicular to the center. The longer one looks at the individual flowers, the more interesting they become.

It appears that this top was pieced in the 1930s and then quilted at a later date by a longarm quilting machine using an overall design. The quilt has been used since that time.

MAKE THE ANTIQUE QUILT

Finished Quilt Size 70" x 80"
Finished Block Size 10¾" x 9¼"
Number of Blocks 44 whole and 8 half

MATERIALS

Based on 42" fabric width.

Assorted print scraps for flowers

Assorted solids for flower centers

Green solid ½ yard

Purple solid 2⅛ yards

White solid 5 yards

Backing 5 yards

Batting 76" x 86"

Coordinating thread

Card stock, freezer paper or heat-resistant Mylar

Rotary-cutting tools

CUTTING INSTRUCTIONS

Refer to Diagram 1 for cutting squares into triangles.

Diagram 1

Scraps

- 6 A pieces of 1 fabric for each flower and 1 solid for center using pattern given on page 110; repeat for 148 flowers.

Green solid

- 148 leaves using pattern given on page 110; add a seam allowance all around when cutting.

Purple solid

- 88 C using pattern given on page 111
- 8 each D and DR using pattern given on page 111
- 64 E using pattern given on page 112

White solid

- 44 B and 8 half B using pattern given on page 110
- 60 F using pattern given on page 112

Use ¼" seam allowance for piecing. Arrows indicate pressing direction.

APPLIQUÉING THE BLOCKS

1. To finish one block, fold and crease each B background piece to find the center (Diagram 2).

Diagram 2

2. Cut 888 card-stock, freezer-paper or Mylar pieces using the pattern for A. *The Mylar shapes can be reused for each flower so you only need to cut 7 shapes. You may also purchase paper or Mylar hexagons cut to size already.* Repeat for leaf shapes using leaf pattern.

3. Fold edges of each of the six print A pieces over the edge of a card-stock, freezer-paper or Mylar piece and press (Diagram 3).

Diagram 3

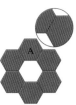

Diagram 4

4. From the top side, hand-stitch the edges of six print A flower pieces together to make a ring (Diagram 4); remove paper.

5. Center the ring on one solid A piece; hand-stitch edges in place (Diagram 5).

Diagram 5

6. Repeat step 3 with leaf pieces.

7. Arrange three flower shapes and three leaf shapes on each B piece referring to Diagram 6 for positioning; baste and then hand-stitch in place. Repeat for 44 blocks.

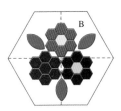

Diagram 6

8. Repeat to complete eight half blocks each with two flowers and two leaves referring to Diagram 7; trim the excess of one flower even with edge of B.

Diagram 7

Block Diagram
10³/₄" x 9¹/₄"
Make 44 whole & 8 half

ASSEMBLING THE TOP

Refer to the Assembly Diagram as needed for the following instructions.

1. Arrange six whole blocks with 10 C pieces and two each D and DR pieces and join to make a row (Diagram 8); press. Repeat for four rows.

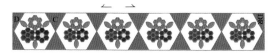

Diagram 8

2. Arrange five blocks with two half blocks and 12 C pieces and join to make a row (Diagram 9); press. Repeat for four rows.

3. Join the rows to complete the quilt center; press seams in one direction.

Diagram 9

4. Join 16 F triangles and 17 E triangles to make a side border strip (Diagram 10); press. Repeat with 14 F and 15 E triangles to make the top and bottom strips; press.

Diagram 10

5. Sew the longer strips to opposite sides and shorter strips to the top and bottom of the quilt center; stitch seam at corners to join triangles. Press the seams of the pieced strips toward the strips and the corner seams open.

FINISHING

1. Piece backing to create a 76" x 86" rectangle.

2. Mark top for quilting, sandwich quilt layers, hand- or machine-quilt and bind edges referring to the General Quiltmaking Instructions.

Hexagon Bouquets
Assembly Diagram 70" x 80"

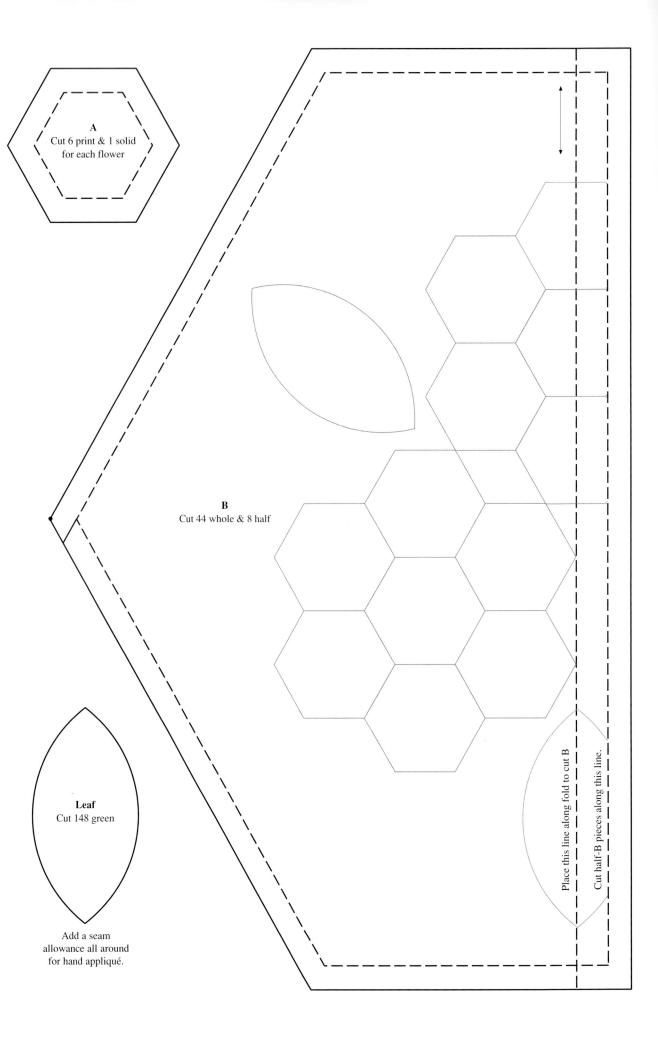

A
Cut 6 print & 1 solid
for each flower

B
Cut 44 whole & 8 half

Leaf
Cut 148 green

Add a seam
allowance all around
for hand appliqué.

Place this line along fold to cut B

Cut half-B pieces along this line.

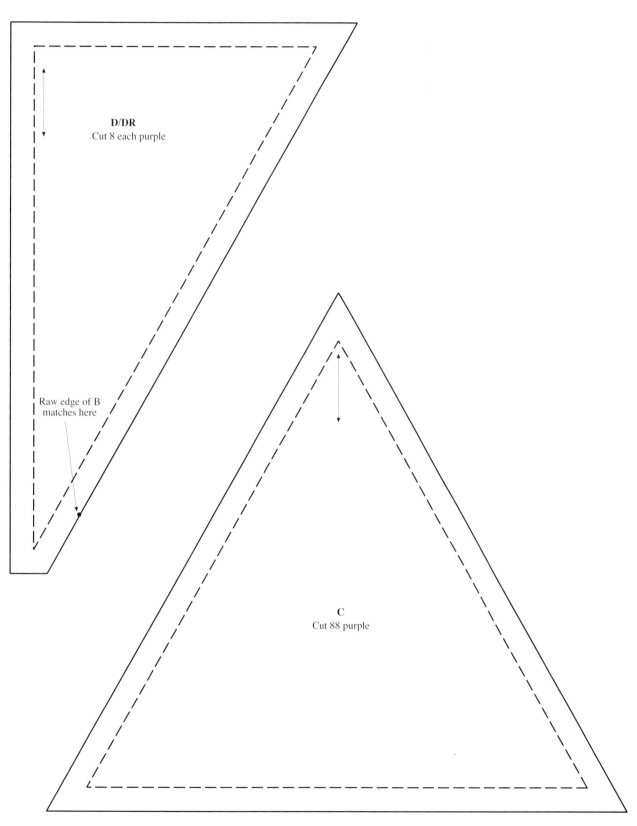

D/DR
Cut 8 each purple

Raw edge of B
matches here

C
Cut 88 purple

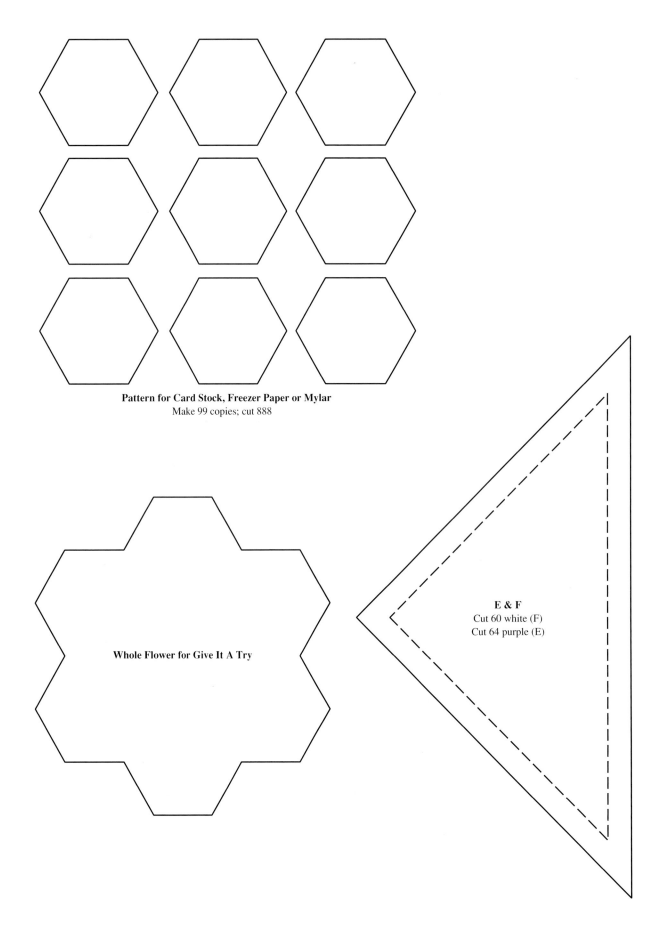

Pattern for Card Stock, Freezer Paper or Mylar
Make 99 copies; cut 888

Whole Flower for Give It A Try

E & F
Cut 60 white (F)
Cut 64 purple (E)

Give It A Try...

There are still quilters who like using the English paper-piecing method, but this takes lots of time that many of us today just don't have. If you like the appearance of this design and want to give it a try using a quicker method, the instructions below are perfect for you.

- Collect scraps for flowers and leaves, 1 yard fusible web and 1 yard fabric stabilizer along with 1 yard cream tonal for the B hexagons and 1/2 yard bright print for the C pieces and border strips.

- Cut 7 B pieces and 12 bright print C pieces.

- Trace 21 each whole flowers, A centers (without the seam allowance) and leaves onto the paper side of the fusible web, leaving spaces between each one. Fuse the shapes to the wrong side of fabrics; cut out on marked lines. Remove paper backing from all pieces.

- Center a flower center on a flower; fuse in place. Repeat for all flowers and flower centers.

- Arrange three flowers and three leaves on each B piece as for quilt; fuse in place. Repeat for seven blocks.

- Cut seven 9" squares fabric stabilizer; pin a square to the wrong side of each fused block.

- Using matching or contrasting thread, machine-stitch around each shape using a narrow zigzag stitch.

- When stitching is complete, remove the fabric stabilizer.

- Join the blocks in rows with C pieces (Diagram 1); press. Join the rows; press.

- Cut six 2 1/2" x 20" strips border fabric; center and sew a strip to every other side of the pieced hexagon top. Press seams toward strips; trim excess even with angled edges. Sew the remaining strips to the remaining sides of the top, trim and press seams toward strips.

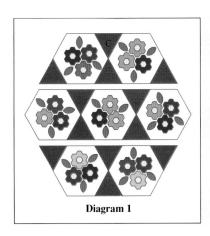

Diagram 1

Hexagon Illusions

The blocks used to create Hexagon Illusions require templates; it is not an easy design to piece. The workmanship on the antique quilt is not good. It is amazing why a quilter with poor skills would take the time and effort needed to finish such a hard project.

When trying to find the name of the block in all of our identification books, this block was unnamed. There was no historical information regarding its origin. The quilt shown was probably made in the 1940s, but we have seen several examples of this quilt made with fabrics from earlier periods. The quilt shown is squared up at the top and bottom, while the sides have bound hexagon edges. The outside points in all the blocks are made with red—red solid, red check, red stripe, red dots. The illusion alluded to in the block name we chose refers to the fact that one shape is used to create the whole design. If you look at the quilt or the block drawing, the two pieces that form the base of each unit don't look like the same shape as the piece that forms the red star point. But it is! Just one template is needed for the whole quilt (Figure 1). The B and C templates are used, however, in our Give It A Try.

This pattern is a challenge and not for beginners. It may be hand-pieced, but it is possible to machine-piece as evidenced in our Give It A Try sample. The secrets to success are accurate marking and stopping stitching at the marks to allow the pivot needed to set a piece into another piece. When setting pieces into others, begin from the outside edges of the pieces, stitch to the marked end of the seam allowance and secure stitching.

Figure 1

MAKE THE ANTIQUE QUILT

Finished Quilt Size 76" Square
Finished Block Size 13¾" x 16"
Number of Blocks 30 whole and 6 half

MATERIALS

Based on 42" fabric width.

Assorted light and dark print scraps

Orange solid ¾ yard

Red fabrics 1½ yards total

Muslin 6 yards

Backing 4¾ yards

Batting 82" square

Coordinating thread

Template material

CUTTING INSTRUCTIONS

Scraps

- Cut 396 A pieces in sets of 12 from each fabric using the template given.

Orange solid—fabric-width strips

- Cut 9 strips 2¼" or 2½" for binding

Red

- Cut 198 A pieces in sets of 6 using the template given; or, cut fourteen 3⅛" fabric-width strips, lay the A template on layered strips and cut multiple pieces using a straight-edge and rotary cutter. Be careful not to trim template when cutting.

Muslin

- Cut 990 A pieces using the template given; or, cut sixty-six 2⅞" fabric-width strips and cut as for red A pieces.

Use ¼" seam allowance for piecing. Arrows indicate pressing direction.

PIECING THE BLOCKS

1. Make a hole in the A template at the corners marked by the black dots using a hole punch; mark the wrong side of each fabric patch placing the tip of a sharp pencil in the hole to make the mark. This mark indicates the end of the seam allowance and is important for matching purposes to indicate the point to stop stitching when setting pieces together.

2. To complete one block, join two same-fabric A pieces, starting stitching on the edge of one seam and stopping stitching at the marked dot at the end of the seam and securing stitching at the beginning and end (Diagram 1).

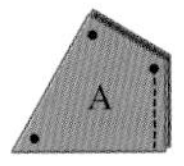

Diagram 1

3. Pin a muslin A piece to the pieced unit, folding one A piece back out of the way (Diagram 2); stitch from the outside edge into the center and stop stitching at the marked point (Diagram 3); repeat on the opposite side to complete one A1 unit (Diagram 4); press. Repeat for six A1 units.

Diagram 2	Diagram 3

A1
Make 6

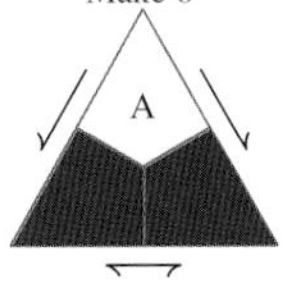

Diagram 4

4. Repeat steps 2 and 3 with one red A and two same-fabric A pieces (of a different fabric than the A1 units) to complete an A2 unit (Diagram 5); press. Repeat for six A2 units.

5. Repeat steps 2 and 3 with one different-fabric A and two muslin A pieces to complete an A3 unit (Diagram 6); press. Repeat for 12 A3 units.

A2
Make 6

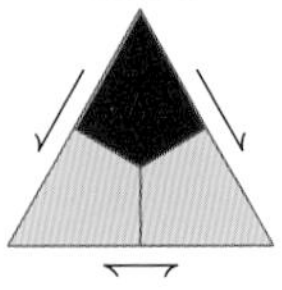

A3
Make 12

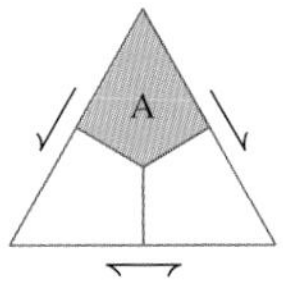

Diagram 5	Diagram 6

6. Sew an A1 unit to an A2 unit (Diagram 7); press. Repeat for six A1-A2 units.

A1

Diagram 7

7. Sew an A3 unit to each side of an A1-A2 unit to complete a star unit (Diagram 8); press. Repeat for six star units.

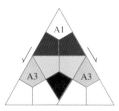

Diagram 8

8. Join three star units to complete half the block, stopping stitching at the marked point of the A1 muslin pieces (Diagram 9); press. Repeat for the second half of the block.

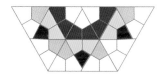

Diagram 9

9. Join the two block halves, starting at the outside edge and stitching to the center; stop stitching and secure. Repeat on the opposite side to the center to complete one block; press seam open. Repeat for 30 blocks.

10. Repeat steps 2-8 to complete six half blocks, making only three each A1 and A2 units and six A3 units.

ASSEMBLING THE TOP

Refer to the Assembly Diagram as needed for the following instructions.

1. Arrange blocks and half blocks in diagonal rows on a flat surface referring to Diagram 10.

Make 2 of each row

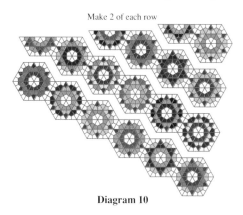

Diagram 10

2. Join the blocks to make diagonal rows referring to the Assembly Diagram for positioning; press seams open.

3. Join the rows, setting one row into the other until the top is complete referring to the Assembly Diagram for positioning of rows.

FINISHING

1. Piece backing to create an 82" square.

2. Mark top for quilting, sandwich quilt layers, hand- or machine-quilt and bind edges referring to the General Quiltmaking Instructions. The quilt shown was hand-quilted 1/4" from seams of all pieces.

Hexagon Illusions
Assembly Diagram 76" Square

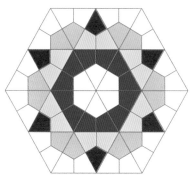

Block Diagram
13³/4" x 16"
Make 30 whole & 6 half

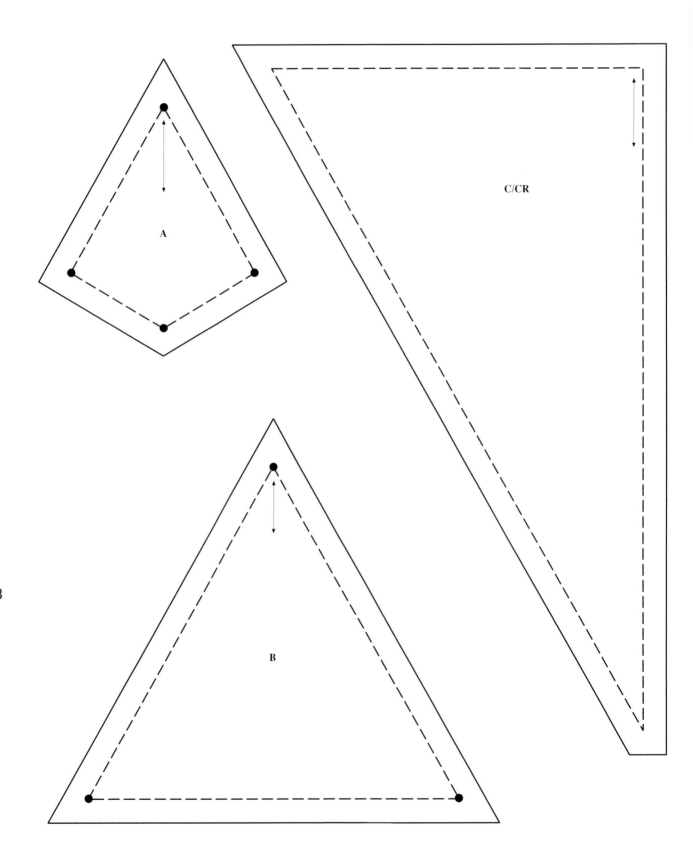

Give It A Try...

The Give It A Try sample eliminates the A3 units in each block; instead piece B is substituted using background fabric. This change in the block highlights the star shape. To make joining the blocks easier, piece C was added to each block to make it a rectangle. With the addition of this piece, the blocks may be stitched in rows and a new design is created.

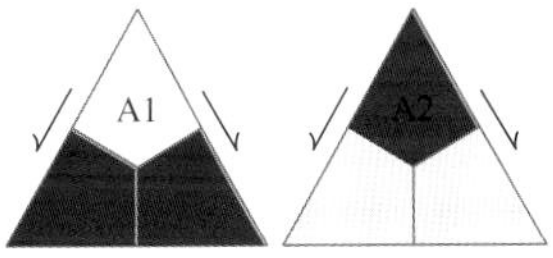

- To give this block a try, select three fabrics: a light, medium and dark. Purchase ½ yard each of the light and medium and 1 yard of dark.
- Prepare the templates for A, B and C.
- Cut 6 light, 12 medium and 18 dark A pieces, 12 light B pieces and two each dark C and CR pieces for each block.
- Stitch six each A1 and A2 units (Diagram 1); press.
- Join an A1 and A2 unit to make an A1-A2 unit as for blocks (Diagram 2); repeat for six units.
- Sew B to each side of each A1-A2 unit to make six star units (Diagram 3); press.
- Join the units as for quilt to complete the hexagon part of the block (Diagram 4); press.

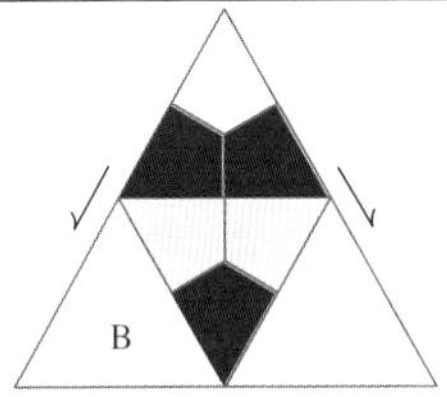

- Sew C and CR to the sides of the block referring to the block drawing to complete a block; press seams toward C and CR. Make four blocks to create the sample.
- Add 1" light, 2" medium and 3" dark borders all around to complete the top as shown.

Diagram 1

Diagram 2

Diagram 3

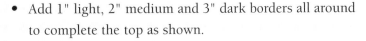

Diagram 4

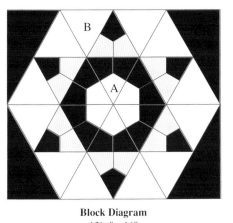

Block Diagram
13¾" x 16"
Make 4

Jacob's Ladder

The indigoes, double pink and shirting fabrics included in this quilt could easily place it in the late 1800s. However according to Barbara Brackman's *Encyclopedia of Pieced Quilt Patterns,* the first known reference to this block was in the *Bureau Farmer,* published by the American Farm Bureau Federation from 1925 to 1935. These kinds of discrepancies often make it difficult to place a date on a quilt without actual documentation from the quiltmaker or her family. Because the quilt uses many different fabrics, it is certainly possible that the quilter delved into her scrap basket and used only those from the late 1800s to early 1900s to make it at some later date. Figure 1 shows the four different indigo prints used in the quilt. The reference to this pattern in the *Bureau Farmer* is only the first reference known today. The pattern may have been developed earlier, but a source has not been found as yet.

Figure 1

This dilemma is a good reason that quilters today should always include a label on their quilts with at least their name, the date when the quilt was made and where it was made. Other information, such as the name of the pattern, the source of the pattern, fabric lines and the reason it was made, could also be included. This will all be of great interest to the collector who 100 years from now may be admiring an "antique" quilt.

MAKE THE ANTIQUE QUILT

Finished Quilt Size 65" x 74"
Finished Block Size 9" Square
Number of Blocks 42

MATERIALS

Based on 42"-wide fabric.

Gold check ½ yard

White solid 1¼ yards

Double pink print 1½ yards

Light prints/stripes 1⅝ yards

Indigo prints 2 yards

Backing 4¾ yards

Batting 71" x 80"

Coordinating thread

Rotary-cutting tools

CUTTING INSTRUCTIONS

Gold check–fabric-width strips

- 6 strips 2" for B

White solid–fabric-width strips

- 12 strips 2" for A

- 7 strips 2¼" for J and K borders

Double pink print–fabric-width strips

- 6 strips 2" for C

- 7 strips 2½" for H and I borders

- 7 strips 2¼" or 2 1/2" for binding

Light prints/stripes–fabric-width strips

- 13 strips 3⅞"; cut into 126-3 7/8" D squares.

Indigo prints–fabric-width strips

- 13 strips 3⅞"; cut into one-hundred-twenty-six 3⅞" E squares.

- 6 strips 2¼" for F and G borders

Use ¼" seam allowance for piecing. Arrows indicate pressing direction.

PIECING THE BLOCKS

1. Draw a diagonal line from corner to corner on the wrong side of each D square.

2. Place a D square right sides together with an E square, stitch ¼" from each side of the drawn line, cut apart on the line and press to complete two D-E units (Diagram 1). Repeat to complete 252 D-E units.

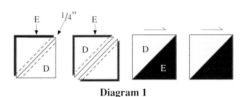

Diagram 1

3. Sew an A strip to a B strip to make an A-B pieced strip (Diagram 2); press. Repeat to make six A-B pieced strips. Repeat with A and C pieced strips to make six A-C pieced strips (Diagram 2).

4. Cut the pieced strips into 126 each A-B and A-C 2" units (Diagram 2).

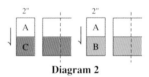

Diagram 2

5. Join two A-B units to make an A-B Four-Patch unit (Diagram 3); press. Repeat for 63 units. Repeat with A-C units to make 63 A-C Four-Patch Units.

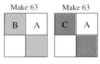

Diagram 3

6. Sew a D-E unit to opposite sides of an A-B unit to make a Block 1 center row (Diagram 4); press. Repeat to make 21 each Block 1 and Block 2 center rows (Diagram 4).

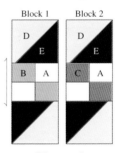

Diagram 4

7. Join a Four-Patch A-B unit with two D-E units to make a Block 1 side row (Diagram 5); press. Repeat to make 42 each Block 1 and Block 2 side rows (Diagram 5).

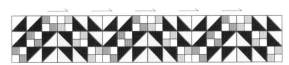

Diagram 5

8. Sew a Block 1 center row between two Block 1 side rows to complete one block referring to Block Diagram 1 for positioning of rows; press seams toward the center row. Repeat to make 21 blocks.

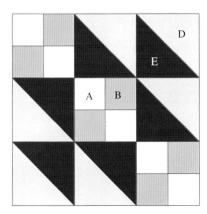

Block Diagram 1
9" Square
Make 21

9. Sew a Block 2 center row between two Block 2 side rows to complete one block referring to Block Diagram 2 for positioning of rows; press seams toward the side rows. Repeat to make 21 blocks.

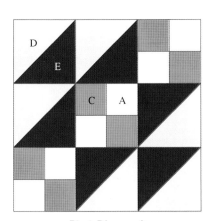

Block Diagram 2
9" Square
Make 21

ASSEMBLING THE TOP

Refer to the Assembly Diagram as needed for the following instructions.

1. Join three of each block to make a row (Diagram 6); press. Repeat to make seven rows.

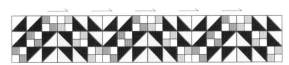

Diagram 6

2. Join the rows to complete the center referring to the Assembly Diagram for positioning of rows; press seams in one direction.

3. Join the F/G strips on short ends to make a long strip; press seams in one direction. Cut into two 63½" F strips and two 58" G strips.

4. Sew the F strips to opposite long sides of the center and the G strips to the top and bottom; press seams toward strips.

5. Join the H/I strips on short ends to make a long strip; press seams in one direction. Cut into two 67" H strips and two 62" I strips.

6. Sew the H strips to opposite long sides and the I strips to the top and bottom; press seams toward strips.

7. Join the J/K strips on short ends to make a long strip; press seams in one direction. Cut into two 71" J strips and two 65½" K strips.

8. Sew the J strips to opposite long sides and the K strips to the top and bottom; press seams toward strips.

FINISHING

1. Piece backing to create a 71" x 80" rectangle.

2. Mark top for quilting, sandwich quilt layers, hand- or machine-quilt and bind edges referring to the General Quiltmaking Instructions.

Jacob s Ladder
Assembly Diagram 65" x 74"

Give It A Try...

Turn the Jacob's Ladder blocks one way to create this star-design sample. Or, turn them another way to create a square-in-a-square design shown here in Diagram 1.

- Referring to quilt Cutting Instructions on page 122, cut 4 A strips, 12 D squares and two borders each 2" x 18½" and 2" x 21½" from light print.

- Cut 2 C strips red print and 2 B strips gold print.

- Cut 12 E squares navy stripe and two borders each 4½" x 24½" and 4½" x 32½" from navy print.

- Complete two of each block referring to Piecing the Blocks on page 122. Cut an additional 15 each A-B and A-C units for border.

- Join one of each block to make a row; repeat for two rows. Press seams toward Block 1.

- Join the rows to complete the center; press seams in one direction.

- Sew the shorter light print borders to opposite sides and the longer strips to the remaining sides; press seams toward strips.

- Join the A-B and A-C units to make four border strips (Diagram 2); press seams away from A pieces.

- Sew the shorter strips to opposite sides and the longer strips to the remaining sides referring to the sample photo for positioning of strips; press seams toward the light border strips.

- Sew the shorter navy print borders to opposite sides and the longer strips to the remaining sides; press seams toward strips to complete the sample.

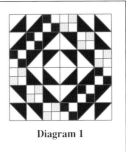

Diagram 1

Diagram 2

Kite Flowers

When searching for the historical name of this block in Barbara Brackman's *Encyclopedia of Pieced Quilt Patterns*, we found this block as Unnamed; we named it Kite Flowers. It was credited to the Old Chelsea Needlecraft Station Needlecraft Services and Alice Brooks. This mail order company, known as Readers Mail, began in 1933 advertising in various periodicals throughout the country. Because orders were sent to the Old Chelsea Station, a post office branch in New York City, the company became known as Old Chelsea Station Needlecraft Service. In addition to quilt patterns, the company sold knit and crochet patterns, embroidery patterns and iron-on transfers. Quilt patterns were published under the names of Alice Brooks, Laura Wheeler and Carol Curtis. The company continues today as an Internet business, but they no longer do many quilting patterns.

The design was shown with all B pieces as one fabric with four different fabrics being used. The version used in this quilt is made with pastel colors except for the blocks on the top and bottom rows. It would appear that the quiltmaker ran out of fabric, but it is curious why the darker green color was chosen (Figure 1). It may be that the blocks were finished by another quilter and joined into the quilt. If the blocks were butted together rather than sashed, the corners of the blocks would come together with 12 points, so sashing is a great option to eliminate the worry of trying to get all those points to match.

Figure 1

MAKE THE ANTIQUE QUILT

Finished Quilt Size 74" x 87"
Finished Block Size 9" Square
Number of Blocks 42

MATERIALS

Based on 42" fabric width.

Light blue solid 1 yard

Light teal 1¾ yards

Print 1½ yards

White solid 5⅛ yards

Backing 5½ yards

Batting 80" x 93"

Coordinating thread

Rotary-cutting tools

CUTTING INSTRUCTIONS

Light blue solid

- 168 B using pattern given on page 129

Light teal solid–fabric-width strips

- 8 strips 3½" for H and I borders
- 2 strips 2½"; cut into thirty 2½" E sashing squares.
- 9 strips 2¼" or 2½" for binding

Print

- 168 A using pattern given on page 130

White solid

- 168 each C and CR using patterns given on page 130

White solid–fabric-width strips

- 5 strips 9½"; cut strips into seventy-one 2½" D sashing strips
- 4 strips 3½" for F borders
- 4 strips 2½" for G borders

Use ¼" seam allowance for piecing. Arrows indicate pressing direction.

PIECING THE BLOCKS

Begin and end stitching on the marked seam allowances for all piecing.

1. Mark the dots on the templates on each fabric piece using a light lead or mechanical pencil to indicate the beginning/end of the seam allowance.

2. Sew B to each side of A (Diagram 1), matching marks at the beginning and end of seams; press. Add another A to the stitched unit to complete a center unit (Diagram 2); press. Repeat for two center units.

Diagram 1

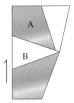
Diagram 2

3. Join two center units to finish the block center (Diagram 3); press seams open.

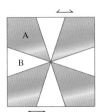
Diagram 3

4. Sew C and CR to opposite sides of B to complete a corner unit (Diagram 4); press. Repeat for four corner units.

Diagram 4

5. Sew a corner unit to each side of the center unit to complete one block; press. Repeat for 42 blocks. *In the quilt shown, 12 blocks are made using green B pieces in the corner units and one block uses three green pieces with one light blue piece in the corner unit. The Assembly Diagram shows the placement of these blocks, but our instructions are given to complete the quilt with all the blocks being the same.*

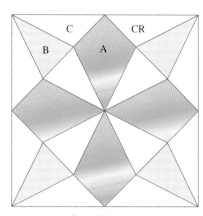

Block Diagram
9" Square
Make 42

ASSEMBLING THE TOP

Refer to the Assembly Diagram as needed for the following instructions.

1. Join six blocks with five D strips to make a block row; press seams toward E. Repeat for seven block rows.

2. Join six D strips with five E squares to make a sashing row; press seams toward E. Repeat for six sashing rows.

3. Join the block rows with the sashing rows; press seams toward sashing rows.

4. Join the F strips on short ends to make a long strip; press seams in one direction. Cut into two 64½" F strips. Sew a strip to the top and bottom; press seams toward F.

5. Join the G strips on short ends to make a long strip; press seams in one direction. Cut into two 81½" G strips; sew a strip to opposite sides. Press seams toward G.

6. Join the H/I strips on short ends to make a long strip; press seams in one direction. Cut into two 81½" H strips and two 74½" I strips. Sew H to opposite sides and I to the top and bottom; press seams toward H and I.

FINISHING

1. Piece backing to create an 80" x 93" rectangle.

2. Mark top for quilting, sandwich quilt layers, hand- or machine-quilt and bind edges referring to the General Quiltmaking Instructions.

Kite Flowers
Assembly Diagram 74" x 87"

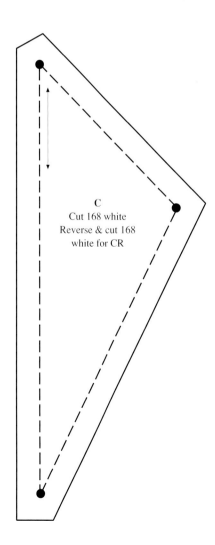

C
Cut 168 white
Reverse & cut 168
white for CR

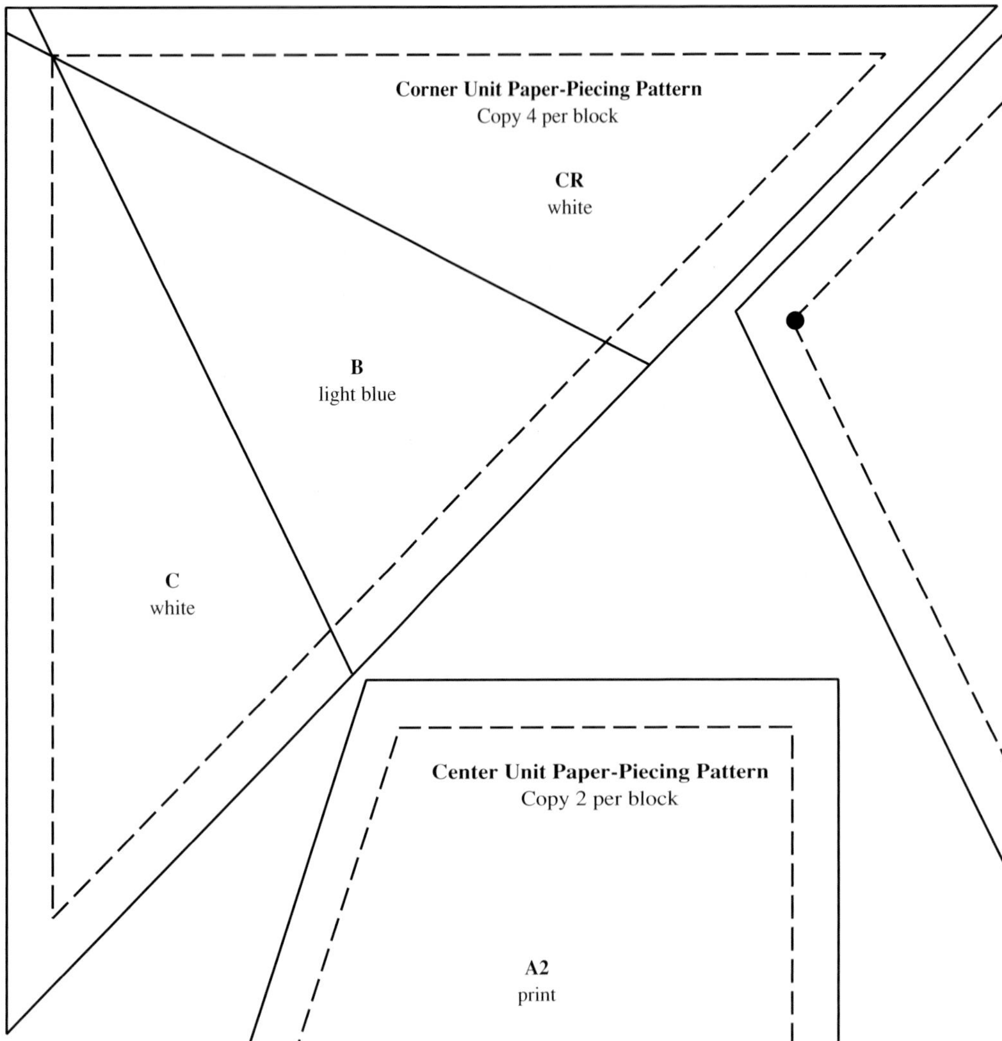

Corner Unit Paper-Piecing Pattern
Copy 4 per block

CR
white

B
light blue

C
white

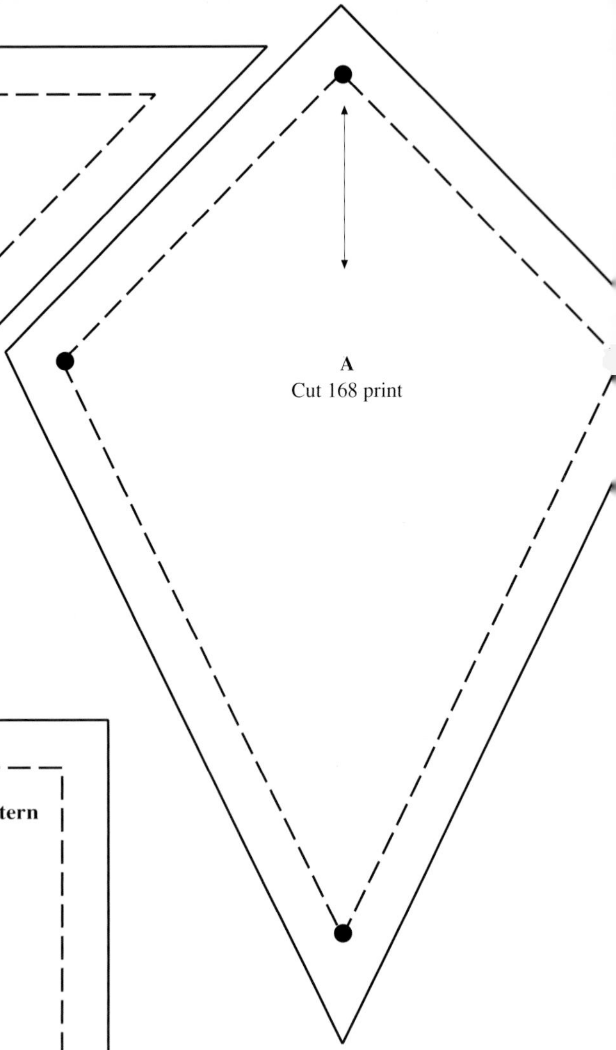

A
Cut 168 print

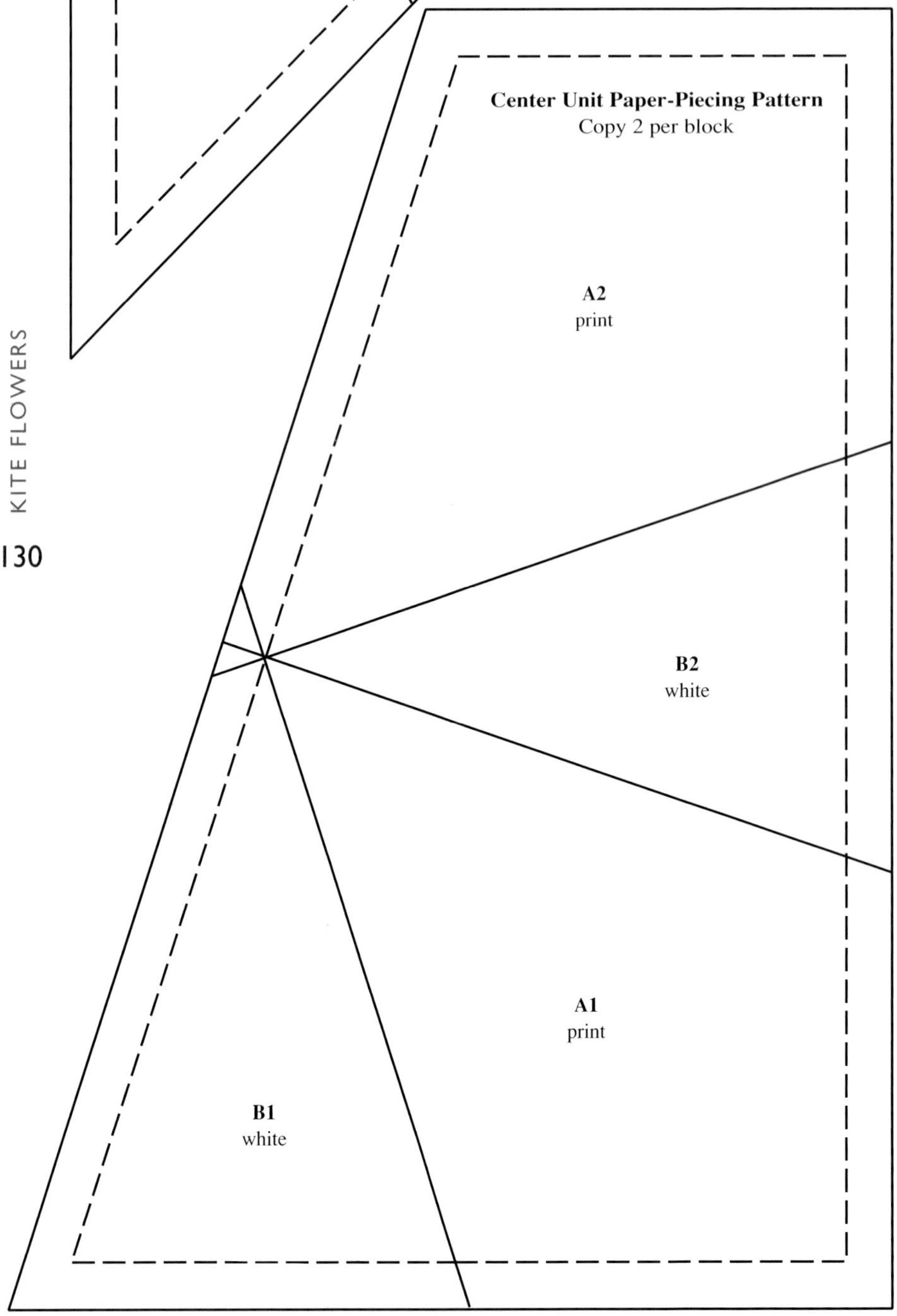

Center Unit Paper-Piecing Pattern
Copy 2 per block

A2
print

B2
white

A1
print

B1
white

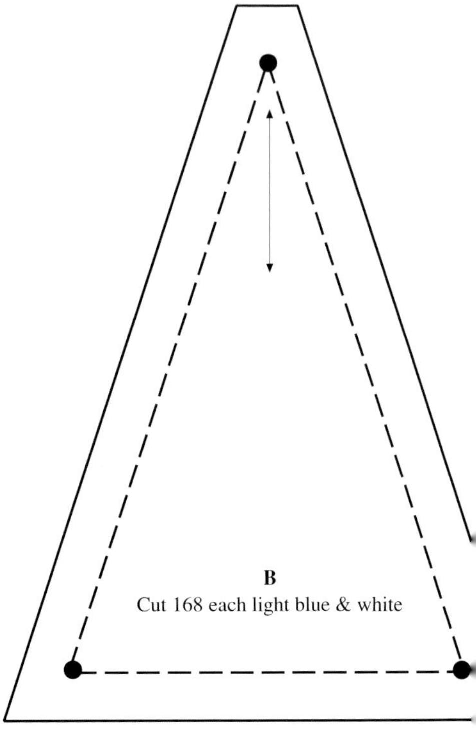

B
Cut 168 each light blue & white

Give It A Try...

Although it is possible to machine-piece the Kite Flower blocks, it is not as easy to get all the points to match perfectly. Hand piecing is an option; paper piecing is another option. The blocks pieced for the sample shown here were paper-pieced. You may use the templates and your rotary cutter to cut the pieces, saving time on the marking/cutting process, although removing the paper takes some time. The advantage is very accurate stitching resulting in seams that match perfectly.

continued on page 132

- Make paper templates for each piece using patterns given. Measure the length of each piece along the grain and cut fabric strips that size.

- Fold a fabric strip to make four aligned layers. Lay the template on the strip, place a rotary ruler on the paper template with the edge of the ruler about 1/16th of an inch beyond the edge of the template and cut. Repeat on all sides to make fabric patches that are the same shape as the original, but a little larger than they would be if they had been cut on the cutting lines. Repeat the process to cut all pieces.

- Make copies of each paper-piecing section; you will need two center units and four corner units for each block. You may photocopy the units to save tracing. Using a window or light box, trace lines onto the other side of the marked paper units to help with placement of pieces, or use a dark marker to mark over lines on the marked side.

- To complete a unit, pin an A1 piece on the unmarked side of one center pattern being sure that the shape exactly covers the whole A1 area (Diagram 1).

- Place a B1 piece right sides together on A1, extending the edge of B1 1/4" beyond the stitching line (Diagram 2); pin on the stitching line between A1 and B1 and unfold B1 to check that after stitching it will cover the B1 area, including the seam allowance. It won't matter if it extends beyond the edges of the paper pattern. Move pins away from stitching line.

- Change stitch length to 20 stitches per inch. Flip the pattern over to the printed side and stitch along the line between A1 and B1, stitching to the outside edges of the pattern (Diagram 3). If aligning pieces is difficult, machine-baste pieces, check for alignment and then stitch in place with the shorter stitch length.

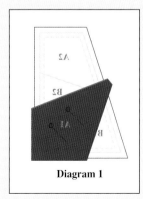

Diagram 1

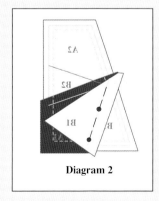

Diagram 2

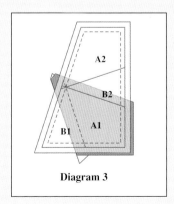

Diagram 3

- Fold the B1 piece over and check that it covers the B1 section (including seam allowances). If so, trim A1-B1 seam allowance to 1/4" (Diagram 4); press B1 to the right side.

- Repeat with B2 on the other edge of A1 and A2 on the edge of B2 (Diagram 5).

- Trim fabric and paper edges even with outer solid line of pattern all around to complete one corner unit. Repeat to make four corner units and two center units per block.

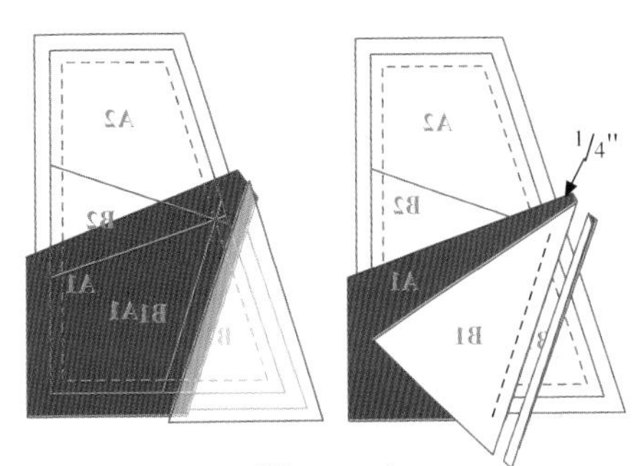

Diagram 4

- Join the units as for quilt to complete a block. Remove the paper backing from the pieced units after they have been stitched into the blocks.

- To frame blocks, cut eight 1 1/2" x 9 1/2" and eight 1 1/2" x 11 1/2" strips dark fabric. Sew the shorter strips to opposite sides of the block; press seams toward strips. Add the longer strips to the top and bottom of the blocks; press seams toward strips.

- Cut nine 2 1/2" squares dark for sashing.

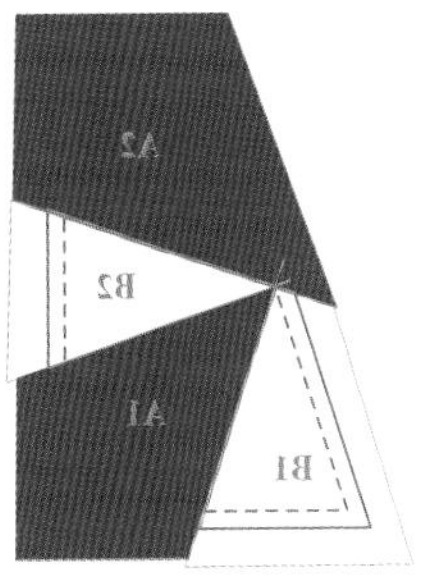

- Cut three stripe strips 2 1/2" by fabric width. Select an area of the stripe for the center of each strip and mark. Center at 5 3/4" and cut an 11 1/2" strip. Repeat for 12 strips. In the sample, the floral violet motifs were chosen as the center stripe and three of these strips were fussy cut from each strip.

Diagram 5

- Join the block with the sashing strips to make two rows of two blocks each; press seams toward strips.

- Join three sashing squares with two sashing strips to make three sashing rows; press seams toward squares.

- Join the rows; press seams toward sashing.

- Cut four 4 1/2" x 28 1/2" strips print and four 4 1/2" squares dark.

- Sew a strip to opposite sides; press seams toward strips.

- Sew a square to each end of the remaining strips; press seams toward strips. Sew these strips to the remaining sides to complete the top.

Potted Posies

In the early 1900s Ann Orr was one of the best-known popular needlework designers in America.
Between 1914 and 1945 in addition to raising three daughters, she published hundreds of
pattern and design booklets and was the editor for two
women's magazines including *Good Housekeeping*, where she
served as needlework editor for 21 years. She had such a
loyal following among readers that well into the 1970s, she
continued to receive mail addressed to her at the magazine.

Figure 1

While she designed in all areas of needlework including knitting,
crocheting, embroidery as well as appliqué and quilting, the
area she seemed to like the best was the block-by-block
design of charts, which she intended to be used for many
different techniques including needlepoint, cross stitch, filet
crochet and quilting.

Her designs were of realistic things, such as flowers, and were graphed and pieced in squares and
triangles (Figure 1). This floral/basket design has similar characteristics. Even the white borders
around the blocks were 1 1/2" squares instead of strips. For ease of piecing, we have combined
some of the squares to make rectangles and strips wherever possible. It is easy to cut all the
pieces using a rotary cutter, but each block includes 57 pieces without the white borders, even
after combining some of the pieces. Our Give It A Try sample shows what a quilt would look
like if each block were pieced with different fabrics, including prints rather than all the same
solid-color fabrics as in the antique version.

MAKE THE ANTIQUE QUILT

Finished Quilt Size 94" x 116"
Finished Block Size 13½" Square
Number of Blocks 12

MATERIALS

Based on 42" fabric width.

Yellow solid ¼ yard

Purple solid ⅜ yard

Orange solid ⅝ yard

Light green solid 1 yard

Green solid 2¾ yards

White solid 7½ yards

Backing 10⅜ yards

Batting 100" x 122"

Coordinating thread

Rotary-cutting tools

CUTTING INSTRUCTIONS

Refer to Diagram 1 for cutting squares into triangles.

Diagram 1

Yellow solid–fabric-width strips

- 3 strips 2" for A

Purple solid–fabric-width strips

- 4 strips 2⅜"; cut into sixty 2⅜" squares. Cut squares in half on 1 diagonal to make 120 I triangles.

Orange solid–fabric-width strips

- 3 strips 2" for B
- 3 strips 3½"; cut into forty-seven 2" C rectangles.

Light green solid–fabric-width strips

- 11 strips 2¼" or 2½" for binding

Green solid

Refer to Diagram 2 for layout suggestion for cutting all green pieces along the length of the fabric.

- seventy-one 2⅜" squares; cut in half on 1 diagonal to make 141 E triangles.
- thirty-six 2½" x 14" R sashing strips
- four 2½" x 18" S sashing strips

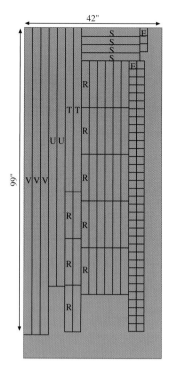

Diagram 2

- four 2½" x 49" T sashing strips
- two 2½" x 78" U sashing strips
- three 2½" x 91½" V sashing strips
- Cut stem pieces referring to patterns

White solid–fabric-width strips

- 4 strips 3½"; cut into sixty-nine 2" D rectangles.
- 4 strips 2"; cut into eighty-three 2" G squares.
- 1 strip 5½"; cut into twelve 3½" H rectangles.
- 8 strips 2⅜"; cut into one-hundred-thirty-one 2⅜" squares. Cut squares in half on 1 diagonal to make 261 F triangles.
- 1 strip 11"; cut into twenty-one 2" J strips.
- 2 strips 14"; cut into thirty-five 2" K strips and three 2" x 11" J strips.
- 1 strip 8"; cut into eleven 2" M strips.
- 1 strip 12½"; cut into eleven 2" N strips.

White solid

Refer to Diagram 3 for layout suggestion for cutting remaining white solid pieces along the remaining length of the fabric.

- nine 5½" squares; cut on both diagonals to make 33 L triangles.
- twenty 13½" O squares

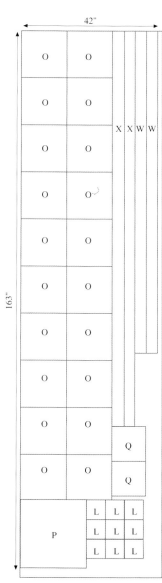

Diagram 3

• one 20⅜" square; cut on both diagonals to make 4 P triangles (set aside 1).

• two 10⅜" squares; cut on 1 diagonal to make 4 Q triangles

• two 3½" x 96" for W borders

• two 3½" x 118" for X borders

Use ¼" seam allowance for piecing. Arrows indicate pressing direction.

MAKING THE BLOCKS

1. To piece one block, sew an A strip to a B strip; press. Repeat for three pieced strips. Cut the pieced strips into forty-seven 2" A-B units (Diagram 4). Set aside 11 units for side units.

Diagram 4

2. Sew C to an A-B unit (Diagram 5); press. Repeat for three A-B-C units.

3. Sew E to F (Diagram 6); press. Repeat for nine E-F units.

4. Sew I to F (Diagram 6); press. Repeat for 10 I-F units.

5. Arrange the pieced units with D, G and H pieces in rows (Diagram 7). Join pieces and units referring to Diagram 8; press seams away from white whenever possible. Join the pieced units in rows; press. Join the rows to complete one block. Repeat for 12 blocks.

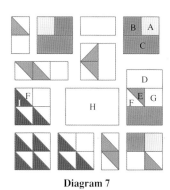

Diagram 5

Diagram 6

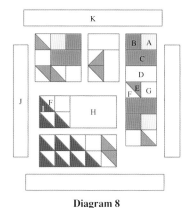

Diagram 7

Diagram 8

6. Prepare stem pieces (on page 140) for appliqué and place on blocks referring to the block diagram for positioning. Hand-stitch in place. Ends of stems may be tucked into seams by unstitching seam areas at ends of stems. After tucking stem ends into opening, re-stitch to secure seams.

MAKING THE SIDE UNITS

1. To piece one side unit, sew an A-B unit to C (Diagram 5); press.

2. Sew E to F (Diagram 6); press. Repeat for three E-F units.

3. Arrange the pieced units in rows with D, G, L and M pieces referring to Diagram 9. M will extend beyond edges of L and will be trimmed.

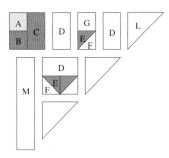

Diagram 9

4. Join the pieces in units to create rows; join the rows to create a side unit, leaving the M piece extended; press.

5. Sew N to one side and K to the adjacent side of the pieced unit, letting ends extend referring to Diagram 10.

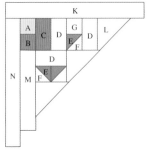

Diagram 10

6. Trim ends of N, K and M at an angle even with L (Diagram 11) to complete a side unit; press. Repeat for 11 side units.

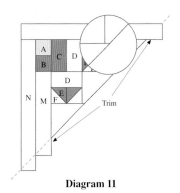

Diagram 11

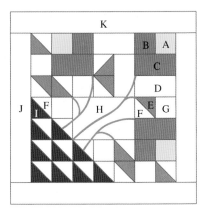

Block Diagram
13¹/₂" Square
Make 12

ASSEMBLING THE TOP

Refer to the Assembly Diagram as needed for the following instructions.

1. Join one side unit, one O square, one P triangle with two R strips and add S and Q to make a top corner unit (Diagram 11); press. Repeat for a reversed top corner unit (Diagram 12). Trim excess S and T even with angled edges again referring to Diagram 12.

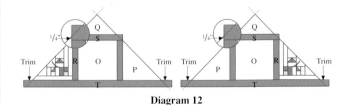

Diagram 12

2. Repeat step 1 with two side units to make two bottom corner units (Diagram 13); press. Trim excess S and T even with angled edges again referring to Diagram 13.

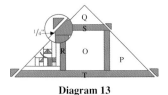

Diagram 13

3. Arrange the remaining side units with the pieced blocks, O squares and R, T, U and V sashing strips referring to Diagram 14. Join to complete rows with R sashing strips, O squares and pieced blocks and side units; press seams toward R.

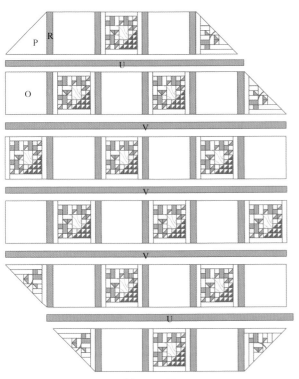

Diagram 14

4. Join the rows with the U and V sashing strips; press seams toward U and V.

5. Add the previously pieced corner units to finish the quilt top assembly.

FINISHING

1. Piece backing to create a 100" x 122" rectangle.

2. Mark top for quilting, sandwich quilt layers, hand- or machine-quilt and bind edges referring to the General Quiltmaking Instructions. The design on page 140 is given for the quilting in the O squares.

Potted Posies
Assembly Diagram 94" x 116"

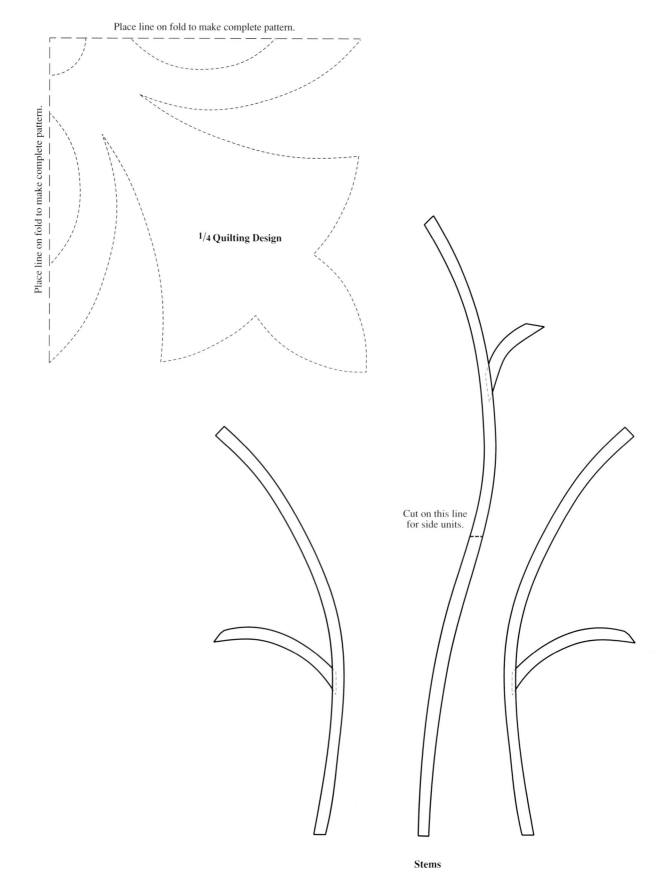

Place line on fold to make complete pattern.

Place line on fold to make complete pattern.

¹/4 Quilting Design

Cut on this line for side units.

Stems
Cut 13 each green solid for blocks
Cut 11 green solid center stems for side units.

Give It A Try...

The Give It A Try sample for this pattern doesn't make any changes to the block piecing from the instructions for the antique quilt. It does change how the blocks are set together and the colors used in the blocks. The quilt used all the same solid fabrics to create the flowers while the sample uses a different fabric for the flowers and baskets in each block. The yellow and green fabrics were consistent in all blocks.

In the Give It A Try sample, the stems were traced onto fusible web, cut out and fused to the finished blocks instead of being hand-stitched in place. The border and sashings strips were made with 2" scrap squares that coordinated with the blocks. The squares were cut and selected at random for order of piecing. It is amazing to see what a difference using some bright-colored fabrics makes to the look of the block. Another option for joining the blocks might be to have the basket portions of the blocks all facing toward the center, making it non-directional: a perfect choice to finish as a topper for a table. This sashed-and-bordered four-block sample would also be a perfect center for a medallion-style quilt.

Wheel of Fortune

Though the Wheel of Fortune block was introduced in the late 1800s, this quilt was probably made after 1925 when the pink solids became popular (Figure 1). The darker of the two pinks in this quilt is often referred to as Taffy Pink and was used extensively in quilts of this period because it blended so well with other colors of the time – Nile and Apple Greens and Dutch Blue. Quilts of this era were usually heavily quilted (Figure 2) and attention given to decorative borders and edges. Scalloped edges are frequently seen, as well

Figure 1

as, lovely floral appliqué borders. The distinctive border treatment of this Wheel of Fortune quilt is something of a combination of the edge and border styles of the time. The appliquéd sawtooth strip adds a beautiful finishing touch to the outer edges of this quilt (Figure 3).

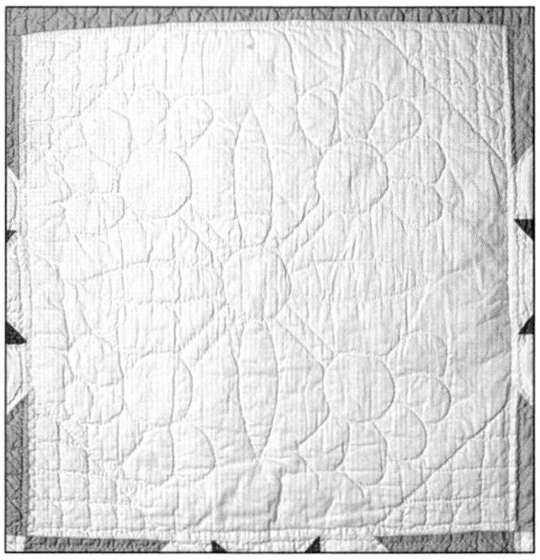

Figure 2

Figure 3

MAKE THE ANTIQUE QUILT
Finished Quilt Size 71" x 85"
Finished Block Size 14¼" Square
Number of Blocks 20

MATERIALS

Based on 42"-wide fabric.

Dark pink solid 1½ yards*

Light pink solid 1⅔ yards

White solid 5 yards

Backing 5½ yards

Batting 77" x 91"

Coordinating thread

Rotary-cutting tools

*The edges of the antique quilt were finished by stitching all around and turning right side out. If you prefer to use binding, purchase 2⅛ yards of dark pink solid instead of 1½ yards.

CUTTING INSTRUCTIONS

Refer to Diagram 1 for cutting squares into triangles.

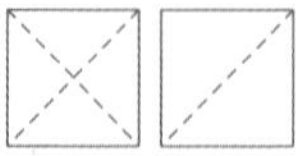

Diagram 1

Dark pink solid–fabric-width strips

- 3 strips 4½"; cut into twenty 4½" squares. Cut squares on both diagonals to make 80 D triangles.
- 4 strips 3⅛"; cut into forty 3⅛" squares. Cut squares on 1 diagonal to make 80 F triangles.
- 8 strips 2½" for sawtooth appliqué
- 8 strips 2¼" or 2½" for binding *(optional)*

Light pink solid–fabric-width strips

- 2 strips 8¼"; cut into ten 8¼" A squares.
- 3 strips 5⅛"; cut into twenty 5⅛" squares. Cut squares on 1 diagonal to make 40 H triangles.
- 3 strips 2⅜" for J borders
- 4 strips 2½" for K borders

White solid–fabric-width strips

- 3 strips 2¾"; cut into forty 2¾" B squares.

- 3 strips 4½"; cut into twenty 4½" squares. Cut squares on both diagonals to make 80 C triangles.
- 3 strips 5¾"; cut into twenty 5¾" squares. Cut squares on both diagonals to make 80 E triangles.
- 2 strips 3⅛"; cut into twenty 3⅛" squares. Cut squares on 1 diagonal to make 40 G triangles.
- 5 strips 14¾"; cut into ten 14¾" I squares.
- 8 strips 5½" for L and M borders

Use ¼" seam allowance for piecing. Arrows indicate pressing direction.

PIECING THE BLOCKS

1. Draw a diagonal line from corner to corner on the wrong side of each B square.

2. Place B right sides together on one corner of A, stitch on the marked line, trim seam allowance to ¼" and press B to the right side (Diagram 2); repeat on each corner of A. Repeat to complete 10 A-B units.

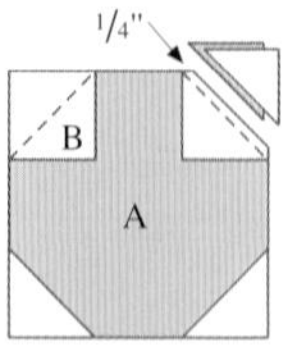

Diagram 2

3. Sew C to D (Diagram 3); press. Repeat to make 80 C-D units.

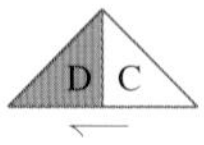

Diagram 3

4. Join two C-D units to make a square (Diagram 4); press. Repeat to make 40 C-D squares.

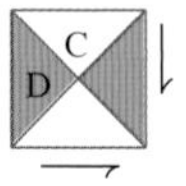

Diagram 4

5. Sew F to one short edge of E (Diagram 5); press. Repeat to make 40 E-F units and 40 reversed E-F units (Diagram 5).

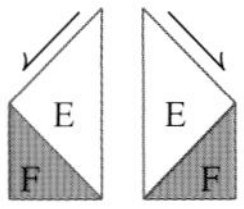

Diagram 5

6. Sew an E-F unit and reversed E-F unit to opposite D sides of a C-D square (Diagram 6); press. Repeat to make 40 pieced strips.

Diagram 6

7. Trim the E points even with the edge of the C-D square (Diagram 7).

Diagram 7

8. Sew a pieced strip to opposite sides of each A-B unit to make 10 block center rows (Diagram 8); press.

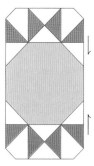

Diagram 8

9. Sew G to each end of the remaining pieced strips to make 20 block side rows (Diagram 9); press.

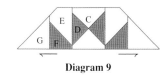

Diagram 9

10. Sew a side row to opposite sides of the block center rows (Diagram 10); press.

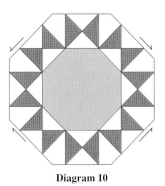

Diagram 10

11. Sew H to each G edge of the pieced units to complete 20 blocks (Diagram 11); press.

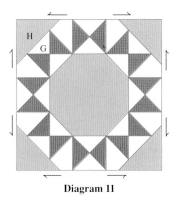

Diagram 11

Block Diagram
14¹/₄" Square
Make 20

ASSEMBLING THE TOP

Refer to the Assembly Diagram as needed for the following instructions.

1. Join two blocks with two I squares to make a row (Diagram 12); press. Repeat to make five rows.

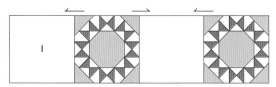

Diagram 12

2. Join the rows to complete the center referring to the Assembly Diagram for positioning of rows; press seams in one direction.

3. Join the J strips on short ends to make a long strip; press seams in one direction. Cut into two 57½" J strips. Sew a strip to the top and bottom of the center; press.

4. Join the K strips on short ends to make a long strip; press seams in one direction. Cut into two 75½" K strips. Sew a strip to opposite long sides of the center; press.

5. Join the L/M strips on short ends to make a long strip; press seams in one direction. Cut into two 61½" L strips and two 85½" M strips. Sew a strip to the top and bottom and then to opposite long sides of the center; press.

6. Use the corner pattern on page 149 to round each corner of the top (Diagram 13).

Diagram 13

ADDING THE SAWTOOTH APPLIQUÉ

1. Join the sawtooth-appliqué strips on short ends to make a long strip; press seams open.

2. Mark 114 sawtooth points on the wrong side of the strip, beginning ¼" from the end of the strip and marking along length (Diagram 14).

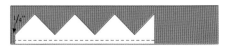

Diagram 14

3. Trim off the unmarked section of strip, leaving ¼" beyond the last sawtooth point (Diagram 15).

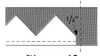

Diagram 15

4. Join the ends of the marked strip; press seam open.

5. Cut out the sawtooth points in a continuous strip, leaving ⅛"-¼" around points for seam allowance (Diagram 16).

6. Turn under seam allowance, clipping into the valley between points (Diagram 17); press or baste to hold.

Diagram 16   **Diagram 17**

7. Pin the sawtooth appliqué strip around the edge of the quilt top, matching raw edges and placing 29 points on each long side, 26 on each end and one in each corner. To fit corner point around curve of corner, make a small pleat on each side of the point (Diagram 18).

Diagram 18

8. Baste strip to quilt top ⅛" from edge.

9. Hand- or machine-stitch the point edge in place.

FINISHING

1. To turn edges in for finishing, piece backing to create a 73" x 87" rectangle. To finish with binding, piece backing to create a 77" x 85" rectangle.

2. Mark top for quilting referring to the General Quiltmaking Instructions. Use the quilting design given on page 148 in the I squares to duplicate the antique quilt.

3. To finish like the antique quilt, place the top right sides together with the backing piece; place the batting piece on bottom. Pin layers to hold; trim backing and batting even with top. Stitch all around edge with a 1/4" seam allowance, leaving a 12" opening on one side. Turn right side out; hand-stitch opening closed. Hand- or machine-quilt to finish.

4. To finish with binding, sandwich quilt layers, hand- or machine-quilt and bind edges referring to the General Quiltmaking Instructions.

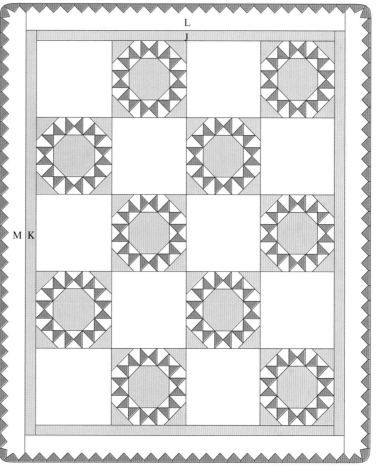

Wheel of Fortune
Assembly Diagram 71" x 85"

Place line on fold to make complete pattern.

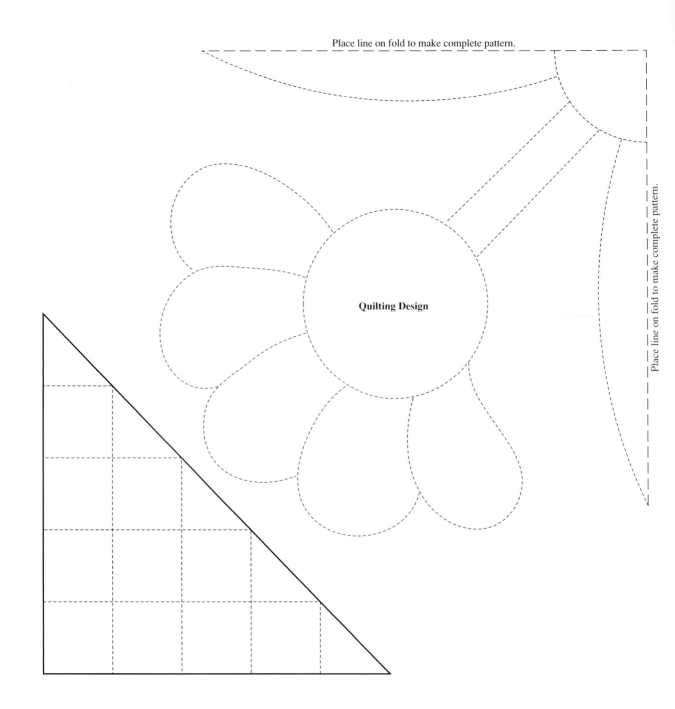

Quilting Design

Place line on fold to make complete pattern.

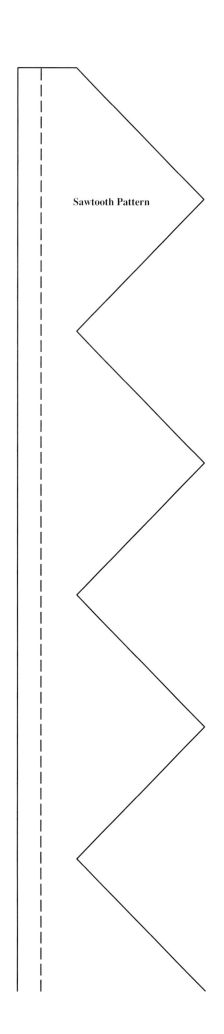

Sawtooth Pattern

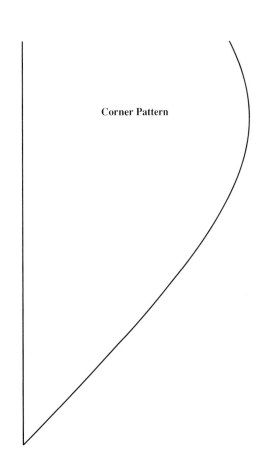

Corner Pattern

Give It A Try...

Add pieced sashing with a pieced border and use a large print to take advantage of the large block centers. Eliminate seam allowances and hand stitching in the sawtooth border appliqué by fusing the strips. You will need 1 yard 18"-wide fusible web for this technique.

- Referring to quilt Cutting Instructions on page 144, cut 4 A squares, one 3¾" K square and two border strips each 7¼" x 36½" and 7¼" x 50" from print.

- Cut 8 D squares, 16 F squares and five 2½" fabric-width sawtooth strips from dark fabric. Cut squares into triangles as needed.

- Cut 8 G squares, four 3¾" x 6¼" J rectangles, four 2⅝" x 4¾" M rectangles and four 2⅝" x 6⅞" N rectangles from light fabric.

- Cut 16 B squares, 8 C squares, 8 E squares, eight 3¾" x 4¾" I rectangles and four 2⅝" x 23¾" L strips from white fabric.

- Cut twelve 2¼" x 18" strips fusible web.

- Complete four blocks referring to Piecing the Blocks on page 144 and the sample photo.

- Sew J between two I strips on the short edges to make a sashing strip; press seams toward J. Repeat to make four strips.

- Join two blocks with one strip; press seams toward strip. Repeat.

- Join the two remaining strips with K; press seams toward strips.

- Join the block rows with the sashing row to complete the center; press seams toward sashing row.

- Sew M to each end of L; press seams toward M. Repeat. Sew the strips to opposite sides of the center; press seams toward strips.

- Sew N to each end of the remaining L strips; press seams toward N. Sew the strips to the remaining sides of the center; press seams toward strips.

- Sew the shorter print border strips to opposite sides and the longer strips to the remaining sides to complete the top: press seams toward strips.

- Join the sawtooth strips on short ends to make a long strip; press seams in one direction. Cut into four 50" strips.

- Bond fusible web along the length of each saw-tooth strip, butting ends of fusible web strips as needed.

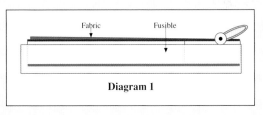

- Trim one long edge of each strip to even fabric and fusible edges (Diagram 1).

Diagram 1

- Mark 18 sawtooth points along length of each strip on the paper side of the fusible web, aligning straight edge of pattern with even edge of strip.

- Cut out sawtooth strips on marked lines; remove paper.

- Center a strip on one outer edge of top, aligning straight edges; fuse in place.

- Place remaining strips on edges of top, overlapping ends of strips with ends of strips on adjacent sides (Diagram 2); fuse in place.

- Machine-stitch along point edge of strips using straight or decorative stitch to complete the sample.

Diagram 2

General Quiltmaking Instructions

FABRIC FOR QUILTMAKING

For several hundred years, quilts were made with 100% cotton fabric, and this remains today the fabric of choice for most quilters.

There are many properties in cotton that make it especially well suited to quiltmaking. There is less distortion in cotton fabric allowing the quilter to accurately join even the smallest bits of fabric. Because a quilt block made of cotton can be ironed flat with a steam iron, any puckered areas can be fixed. The sewing machine needle can move through cotton with a great deal of ease when compared to some synthetic fabrics.

For years, quilters were advised to prewash all of their fabric to test for colorfastness and shrinkage. Now most quilters don't bother to prewash, but they do pre-test. Cut a strip about 2" wide from each piece of fabric that you will use in your quilt. Measure both the length and the width of the strip. Then immerse the strip in a bowl of very hot water, using a separate bowl for each piece of fabric.

Be especially concerned about reds and dark blues because they have a tendency to bleed if the initial dyeing was not done correctly. If it's one of your favorite fabrics that is bleeding, you might be able to salvage the fabric. Try washing it in very hot water until you've washed out all of the excess dye. Unfortunately, fabrics that continue to bleed after they have been washed repeatedly will bleed forever. So, eliminate them right at the start.

Now, take each one of the strips and iron it dry using a hot iron. Be especially careful not to stretch the strip. When the strips are completely dry, measure and compare them to your original strip. If all of your fabric is shrinking the same amount, you don't have to worry about uneven shrinkage in your quilt. When you wash the final quilt, the puckering that will result will give you the look of an antique quilt. If you don't want this look, you are going to have to wash and dry all of your fabric before you start cutting. Iron the fabric, using some spray starch or sizing to give the fabric a crisp finish.

If you are never planning to wash your quilt, i.e. your quilt is intended to be a wall hanging, you could eliminate the pre-testing process. You may run the risk, however, of some future relative to whom you have willed your quilts deciding that the wall hanging needs freshening by washing.

Before beginning to work, make

sure that your fabric is absolutely square. If it is not, you will have difficulty cutting perfectly square pieces. Fabric is woven with crosswise and lengthwise threads. Lengthwise threads should be parallel to the selvage (that's the finished edge along the sides; sometimes the fabric company prints its name along the selvage), and crosswise threads should be perpendicular to the selvage. If fabric is off grain, you can usually straighten it by pulling gently on the true bias in the opposite direction to the off-grain edge. Continue doing this until the crosswise threads are at a right angle to the lengthwise threads.

CUTTING METHODS

Templates

For most of the quilts in this book, we have used rotary cut strips and quick sewing techniques. For a few of the quilts, however, we use traditional templates such as this one.

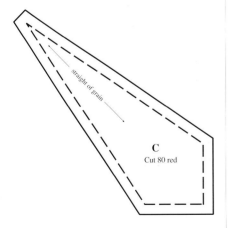

A template is like a dress pattern piece. It tells you exactly how to make the appropriate pattern.

Carefully trace the template piece and then glue it onto heavy cardboard or plastic. (Special plastic for making templates is available in quilt shops or departments.) Transfer all of the lines and written material to the finished template.

Some of the patterns use reverse pieces, which are marked with an R after the pattern letter. Here is a pattern with a reverse template indicated. To reverse the template, simply cut the piece first with the template up; then turn the template over, and cut the piece with the template down. The two pieces will be mirror images of each other.

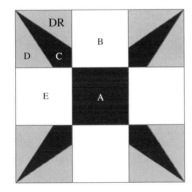

Rotary Cutting

The introduction of the rotary cutter to the quilting world has made all the difference in quilt making today. With rotary cutting you can make quilts faster and with greater accuracy without the use of templates. Instead the pieces are cut into strips and

then the strips are cut into other shapes.

For rotary cutting, you will need three important tools: a rotary cutter, a mat and an acrylic ruler. There are many different brands and types currently on the market. Choose the ones that you feel will work for you.

Don't attempt to use a rotary cutter without an accompanying protective mat. The mat will not only protect your table from becoming scratched, but it will protect your cutter as well. Most mats are self-healing and will not dull the cutting blades. Mats are available in many sizes, but if this is your first attempt at rotary cutting, an 18" x 24" mat is probably the best choice.

A must for cutting accurate strips is a strong straight edge, and acrylic rulers are the perfect choice for this. There are many different acrylic rulers on the market, and they come in several widths and lengths. Either a 6"x 24" or a 6" x 12" ruler will be the most useful. The longer ruler will allow you to fold your fabric only once while the smaller size will require folding twice. Make sure that your ruler has 1/8" increment markings in both directions plus a 45° marking.

Cutting Strips

Before beginning to work, iron your fabric to remove the wrinkles. Fold the fabric in half, lengthwise, bringing the selvage edges together with lengthwise grain aligned.

Fold in half again. Make certain that there are no wrinkles in the fabric.

Now place the folded fabric on the cutting mat.

Place the fabric length on the right side if you are right handed.

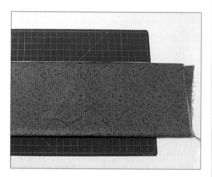

If you are left-handed place the fabric on your left.

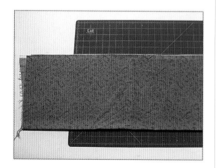

The fold of the fabric should line up along one of the grid lines printed on the mat.

Straighten one of the cut edges first. Lay the acrylic ruler on the mat near the cut edge; the ruler markings should be even with the grid on the mat. Hold the ruler firmly with your left hand

(or, with your right hand if you are left-handed). To provide extra stability, keep your small finger on the mat. Now hold the rotary cutter with the blade against the ruler and cut away from you in one quick motion.

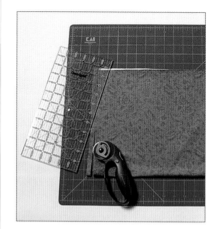

Place the ruler on the required width line along the cut edge of the fabric and cut the strip, making sure that you always cut away from you. Cut the number of strips called for in the directions.

After you have cut a few strips, check to make certain that your fabric continues to be perfectly square. If necessary, re-square the fabric. If you fail to do this, your strips may be bowed with a "v" in the center causing your piecing to become inaccurate as you continue working.

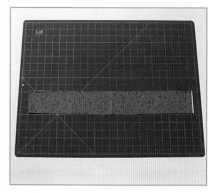

Cutting Squares and Rectangles

Place a stack of strips on the cutting mat. You will be more successful in cutting – at least in the beginning – if you work with no more than four strips at a time. Make certain that the strips are lined up very evenly. Following the instructions given for the quilt, cut the required number of squares or rectangles.

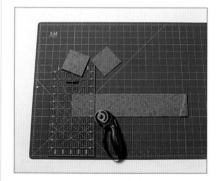

Cutting Triangles

There are a number of different triangle constructions used in the quilts in this book including Half-Square Triangles, Quarter-Square Triangles and Triangle Squares.

The short sides of a Half-Square Triangle are on the straight grain of the fabric. This is especially necessary if the short edges are on the outer edge of the block. Cut the squares the size indicated in the instructions, then cut the square in half diagonally.

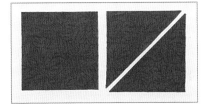

Quarter-Square Triangles are used when the long edge of the triangle must be on the straight grain. This is important when the long edge is on the outside of the block. Again cut the squares the proper size; then cut diagonally into quarters.

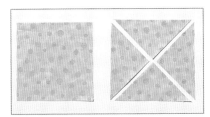

Triangle Squares are squares made up of two different-colored triangles. To make these squares, you can cut individual triangles as described in Half-Square Triangles. Then sew two triangles together. A quick method, especially if you need

several triangle squares with the same fabric, is to sew two squares together. Draw a diagonal line on the wrong side of the lighter square. Place two squares right sides together and sew 1/4" from each side of the drawn line. Cut along the drawn line, and you have created two Triangle Squares.

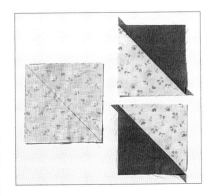

Strip Piecing

This is a much faster and easier method of making quilts rather than creating the blocks piece by piece. With this method, two or more strips are sewn together then cut at certain intervals. For instance, if a block is made up of several 3" finished-size squares, cut 3 1/2"-wide strips along the crosswise grain.

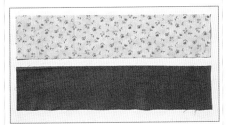

With right sides together, join two strips along the length. The seam should be pressed toward the dark fabric.

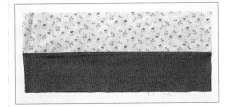

Square one end of the pieced strip and cut along its length at 3 1/2" intervals to create pairs of 3 1/2" squares.

Paper Piecing

Several of the quilts in this collection use a method called paper piecing. In this method, you piece right on a paper pattern, and you do not have to cut exact pieces for the block. Just be sure that each fabric piece is at least 1/4" larger on all sides than the space it is to cover.

The paper-piecing pattern is given with the instructions for a specific quilt.

Trace the block pattern onto your choice of foundation material. Use plain white paper or one of the "disappearing" foundation materials currently on the market.

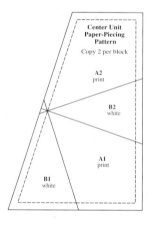

Be sure to include all markings and numbers.

Turn your foundation with the unmarked side facing you and place the first fabric piece right-side up over the proper space on the foundation. You may want to hold your foundation up to a light source such as a window to make sure that the fabric is overlapping at least 1/4" on all sides.

Pin (or use a glue stick) to hold this first fabric piece in place.

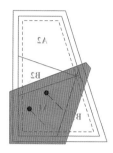

Place the next piece right sides together on the first piece and pin in place. You may want to fold the second piece over to check that it is covering the foundation space.

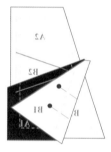

Place the pinned section on the sewing machine with the marked side of the foundation up, making sure that the pieces are in place, and sew along the line between the first two spaces, using a small stitch (about 18 to 20 stitches per inch).

Turn the foundation over; open the second piece and press the seam.

Then turn the foundation with the marked side facing you, fold the foundation forward along the stitched line and trim the fabric about 1/8" to 1/4" from the fold.

In this manner continue sewing and trimming pieces until the block is finished. After you have finished sewing a block, do not remove the paper unless you stay stitch around the outside of a block, or until you have completed your quilt.

ADDING BORDERS

Borders are often added to the top and bottom of a quilt, serving to frame the quilt just as a frame does with a picture.

If you are planning to add borders to your quilt, measure your quilt top lengthwise through the center and cut two border strips to that length by the width measurement given in the instructions. Sew both strips to the sides of the quilt.

Now measure the quilt crosswise through the center, being sure to include the measurement of the borders you have just added. Cut two border strips following the width measurement given in the instructions.

Add these borders to the top and bottom of the quilt. Repeat this process for any additional borders. Use a 1/4" seam allowance at all times and press all of the seams to the darker side. Press the quilt top carefully.

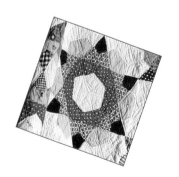

PLANNING THE QUILTING DESIGN

Whether you plan to hand- or machine-quilt your project, you will need to decide how you are going to do the actual quilting.

One of the easiest ways to quilt is to "Quilt in the Ditch," which is a term used to describe stitching along the seam line between two pieces of fabric. Using your fingers, pull the blocks or pieces apart slightly and stitch right between the two pieces. The stitching will look better if you keep the stitching to the side of the seam that does not have the extra bulk of the seam allowance under it. You do not have to mark your top for "in the ditch" quilting. This type of quilting is a favorite of machine quilters.

Another favorite of machine quilters that does not have to be marked on the quilt top is Freeform or Meander quilting. You can use this to fill in open spaces or to quilt around a design or motif. The quilting is done with a darning foot and the feed dogs down on the sewing machine. It takes practice to master Freeform quilting because you are controlling the movement of the quilt under the needle rather than the sewing machine moving the quilt. You can quilt in any direction – up and down, side to side and even in circles – without pivoting the quilt around the needle. Practice this quilting method before trying it on your quilt.

For other quilting patterns, you will need to transfer the quilting design onto your quilt.

While there are quilt marking pencils available at quilt shops or departments, you can use a regular well-sharpened hard lead pencil (using a light-color marking pen for dark fabrics and a regular pencil for light fabrics). Whatever marking tool you choose, be sure to test all marking materials to make certain that they will not run when wet, and that they will disappear when your quilting is complete.

Once you have decided on your quilting plans, and you have marked the top of your quilt, it is ready for the batting and backing.

SANDWICHING THE QUILT LAYERS

There are a number of different types of batting on the market today including the new fusible battings that eliminate the need for basting. Your choice of batting will depend on how you are planning to finish your quilt. Batting made with a thin cotton or cotton/polyester blend works best for machine quilting. Batting with a minimum of scrim binders works best for hand quilting. Very thick polyester batting should be used only for tied quilts.

The best fabric for quilt backing is 100% cotton fabric. If your quilt is larger than the available fabric, you will have to piece your backing fabric. When joining the fabric, try not to have a seam going down the center. Instead cut off the selvages and make a center strip that is about 36" wide and have the narrower strips at the sides. Seam the pieces together and carefully iron the seams open. (This is one of the few times in making a quilt that a seam should be pressed open.) Several fabric manufacturers are now selling fabric in 90" or 108" widths for use as backing fabric.

The batting and the backing should be cut about two to three inches larger on all sides than the quilt top. Place the backing wrong side up on a flat surface. Smooth out the batting on top of this, matching the outer edges. Center the quilt top, right side up, on top of the batting.

Now the quilt layers must be held together before quilting, and there are several methods for doing this:

Thread Basting:
Baste the three layers together with long stitches. Start in the center and sew toward the edges in a number of diagonal lines.

Safety-pin Basting:
Starting from the center and working toward the edges, pin through all layers at one time with large safety pins. The pins should be placed no more than 4" apart. As you work, think of your quilting plan to make sure that the

pins will avoid prospective quilting lines.

Quilt-gun Basting:
This handy trigger tool pushes nylon tags through all layers of the quilt. Start in the center and work toward the outside edges. The tags should be placed about 4" apart. You can sew right over the tags, which can then be easily removed by cutting them off with scissors.

Spray or Heat-set Basting:
Several manufacturers have spray adhesives available especially for quilters. Apply these products by following the manufacturers' directions. You might want to test these products before you use them to make certain that they meet your requirements.

Fusible Iron-on Batting:
These battings are a wonderful new way to hold quilt layers together without using any of the other time-consuming methods of basting. Again, you will want to test these battings to be certain that you are happy with the results. Follow the manufacturers' directions.

ATTACHING THE BINDING

Once the quilt has been quilted, the edges must be bound. Start by trimming the backing and batting even with the quilt top. Machine-baste the three layers together approximately 1/8" from the edge.

Bindings may be made with bias or crosswise fabric strips. Cut bias strips across the diagonal of the fabric and crosswise strips across the fabric width. Bias binding may be purchased in packages at your local fabric store or department, but using self-made binding allows you to use fabric from the quilt.

Measure the quilt top and cut enough 2 1/4" or 2 1/2" wide strips to go around all four sides of the quilt plus 12". Join the strips end to end with diagonal seams and trim the corners.

Press the seams open, Cut one end of the strip at a 45° angle and press under 1/4".

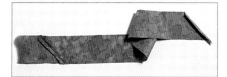

Press the entire strip in half lengthwise wrong sides together.

On the front of the quilt, position the binding in the middle of one side, keeping the raw edges together. Sew the binding to the quilt with 1/4" seam allowance, beginning about 3" below the folded end of the binding.

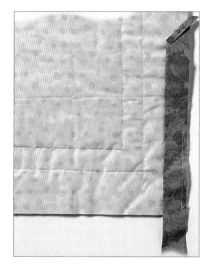

At the corner, stop 1/4" from the edge of the quilt and backstitch.

Fold the binding away from the quilt so that it is at a right angle to the edge just sewn. Then, fold the binding back on itself so the fold is on the quilt edge, and the raw edges are aligned with the adjacent side of the quilt. Begin sewing at quilt edge.

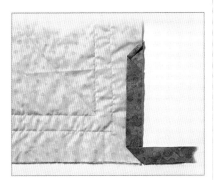

Continue in the same way around the remaining sides of the quilt. Stop about 2" away from the starting point. Trim any excess binding and tuck it inside the folded end. Finish the stitching.

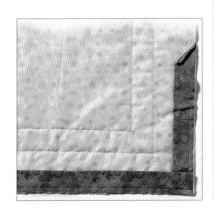

Fold the binding to the back of the quilt so that the seam line is covered; hand-stitch the binding in place on the back of the quilt.

After you have finished making your quilt, always sign and date it for future generations. If the quilts in this book had been signed and dated, we would not have had to guess when they were made.

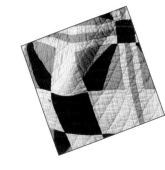

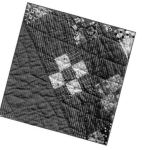

Index